Let Me Count the Ways

Practical Innovations for Jewish Teachers

Carol Oseran Starin

TORAH AURA PRODUCTIONS

All royalites from this book will become part of the
Starin Family Philanthropic Fund of The Jewish Community
Endowment, Seattle Washington
for the support of Jewish education

LIBRARY OF CONGRESS CATALOGING-IN-PUBLICATION DATA

Starin, Carol Oseran, 1945–

Let me count the ways: practical innovations for Jewish teachers / Carol Oseran Starin.

   p.   cm.

   Includes bibliographical references

   ISBN 0-933873-97-2 (alk. paper)

   1. Jewish religious education of children Handbooks, manuals, etc. 2. Judaism—Study and teaching Handbooks, manuals, etc. 3. Classroom management Handbooks, manuals, etc. 4. Teaching Handbooks, manuals, etc. I. Title.

   BM103.S73   1999

   296.6'8—dc21   99-36310

                                     CIP

TORAH AURA PRODUCTIONS • 4423 FRUITLAND AVENUE, LOS ANGELES, CA 90058

(800) BE-TORAH • (800) 238-6724 • (323) 585-7312 • FAX (323) 585–0327

E-MAIL <MISRAD@TORAHAURA.COM> • VISIT THE TORAH AURA WEBSITE AT
WWW.TORAHAURA.COM

MANUFACTURED IN THE UNITED STATES OF AMERICA

Table of Contents

Seventy-five Things for Holiday Celebrations

Forty Ways to Enrich the Teacher in You

Forty-one Things About Using Torah Aura Materials

Bibliography

Many Thanks

There has been a community of people who have shared their knowledge and visions to make the "Let Me Count the Ways" column live from week to week.

Special thanks to: Judy Miller, Susan Fish, Dan Bender, Debbie Findling, Linda Kirsch, Joel Lurie Grishaver, Paul Epstein, Joanne Glosser, Dorothy Glass, Amy Azaroff, Rivy Poupko Kletenik, Julie Katz, Debi Rowe, Iris Petroff, Idie Benjamin, Sue Littauer, Mike Fixler, Adina Hamick, Rabbi Kerry Olitsky, Faye Tillis Lewy, Rabbi Elana Zaiman, Rabbi David Fine, Dodi Christy, Gayle Carrol, Rebecca Alexander, Jennifer Goldberg, Rabbi Aryeh Blaut, Brad Lakritz, Sharon Morton, Drora Arussy, Deena Bloomstone, Marcia Goren Weser, Marla Gamoran, Bina Guerrieri, Yeshaya Kletenik, Danny Siegel, Leslie Mirchin, Tamara Cohen, David Sabban, Tina Rappaport, Bunnie Piltch, Lynn Hazan, Janice Stein, Jane Golub, Rabbi Jerry Kane, Leora Zeitlin, Judy Podolsky, Maria Erlitz, Debby Kerdeman, Beth Huppin, Joyce Shane, Terry Kalet, and Donna Gordon Blankinship.

And special thanks to all of my teachers—and all of those who have inspired me.

Foreword

Jewish teachers have a new best friend and her name is Carol Starin! A Jewish educator of incredible skill and sensitivity, Carol has collected her popular columns of advice for Jewish teachers into this outstanding new book, destined to become the Jewish teachers' Bible. It is a masterful achievement by a masterful teacher.

Carol speaks from real experienced, honed by many years as a classroom teacher, principal and Bureau of Jewish Education executive. She has her ear finely tuned to the "small moments" of teaching that make all the different between a good teacher and a great teacher. In one column, she offers terrific suggests for an often-overlooked challenge—the *second* day of class. In another, she offers five great ways to *end* a lesson. In yet another, she advises teachers about how to interact with "a child who as two homes," sensitively outlining techniques for getting to know both parents and for avoiding language embarrassing to the child.

This is the stuff of real pedagogy, those "best practices" that expert teachers learn over the years and that novice teachers especially need to learn. Carol has wisely included advice from a network of expert teacher who generously share their best "tips" on everything from classroom management to lesson planning. For the beginner or volunteer teacher in any Jewish classroom, supplementary or day school, formal or informal, reading this book is like having a team of the best Jewish educators in the world standing next to you in front of the class, whispering in your ear the best advice for handling just about any situation you can imagine!

Carol Starin's marvelous book should be on every Jewish teacher's desk and required reading in every Jewish teacher preparation program. Every principal of every Jewish school would be well advised to present a copy of *Let Me Count the Ways* to every teacher on the staff. It will be a cherished gift and a phenomenal resource that will be used again and again. Carol and her friends at Torah Aura Productions are to be congratulated for a contribution to the field of Jewish education that will significantly improve the quality of teaching in Jewish schools in the twenty-first century.

Dr. Ron Wolfson
Vice President, Director, Whizin Center for the Jewish Future
Fingerhut Assistant Professor of Education
University of Judaism

Five Secret Tales of Jewish Teaching

Thursdays are my crazy day. It is the day my column is due. It is the day that I know that my "Five Things" column will be late—because they always come down to the wire. The column was designed to serve as a quick resource for teachers and principals, to serve as a quick fix of inspiration and enrichment for classrooms. Every week I collect practical ideas. One week it is five ways to line students up. Another week it is five ways to write a lesson plan. Almost none of the ideas is mine. Some come from my teachers. Some come from my colleagues. Some are collected from a network of contributors who e-mail in their thoughts. Some come from an ever-expanding library of other teachers' "idea" books.

My colleague Gail Dorph, who usually works with grand educational visions, is fond of the statement: "What does that look like?" Her constant task is to turn the theoretical into applicable models. Every week, in the little microcosms in which most teachers work, I ask the same question. Given a problem, what would five solutions look like? Given an opportunity, what picture can we make of five different ways of taking advantage of it? In a certain sense, my five things column is a scrapbook of visions of the baby steps out of which great teaching really actualizes itself: bulletin boards and individual questions, haroset recipes and transitional activities. What I have learned in my years of working with teachers is that the work of the classroom is not only innovative master strategies but well-placed steps that move us through those plans. Teachers plan and act on the micro level as well as on the macro. We have our own best practices for each and every classroom task—and often these practices add up to our ultimate classroom successes.

The reality is that we never know what our students are really learning. We can plan for retention, but we never know what our students remember. We're never sure what really impacts them—or their parents. In our highly mobile society those of us who teach young children may never see them grow up and know them as adults. (And we're not sure where our future teachers are hiding.) Teaching is a very fragile process.

5 Success Stories

1 *Maria Erlitz (1997):* As vice-principal of The Jewish Day School of Metropolitan Seattle, I was asked to interview the former CEO of an educational software company. Recognizing the name, I realized that I had taught this woman's child in religious school many years earlier. I saw her very infrequently back then, so I doubted that she would remember me. As I introduced myself to her she said, "Of course I remember you! You invited all the families into your sukkah, and we celebrated Sukkot with our children."

2. *Dan Bender, a Jewish educator in Honolulu:* "Our temple sanctuary walls are covered with memorial plates from front to back, and the weekly yahrzeits are lighted up with small bulbs. On Sunday mornings we have our weekly religious school assembly, and the children file in after their morning projects. One Sunday I was trying to get the children to sit in the front rows, and I noticed a third-grade girl sitting near to the last row. I told her to move up front with the rest of her class, but she said she wanted to stay where she was. I asked, 'How come?' She pointed to the plaque on the wall near the forty-ninth row and said, 'This is where my grandma is.'"

3. *Faye Tillis Lewy:* "Years ago when I was teaching kindergarten, one of my students came into class anxious to tell me something. 'I know why you're such a good teacher,' he said. 'Oh?' I replied. 'You know that prayer that we say after the Sh'ma? The one that says you should teach "very gently unto the children"? Well, I think you always teach very gently.'"

4. *My Story:* "When I was sixteen, a high school junior at Temple de Hirsch (no Sinai then), the principal asked me to be a 'cadet' teacher. That was not at all what interested me; but there was a boy in that cadet program who did interest me. And it paid $2.50 a week. We not only worked in classrooms, we met together for weekly study. I was assigned to a first-grade class where the teacher 'let me teach.' It was a big year. I learned that I was meant to be in a classroom. (And that boy married me.) Recently one of my former students became the chair of my board."

5. *Maria Erlitz* again: "Our son Corey was in pre-school. We didn't belong to a synagogue and decided to spend Rosh ha-Shanah at Mt. Rainier. We couldn't wait to tell Corey. After all, Mt. Rainier was the most beautiful place anyone could be. Corey came home from the JCC pre-school and listened as we excitedly told him about the Rosh ha-Shanah plans. Really upset and disappointed, he said, 'But I have to hear the shofar. My teacher said that on Rosh ha-Shanah we have to hear the shofar.' So instead of going to the mountain we took him to the nearest synagogue to hear the shofar. We joined the synagogue, and I later became a teacher in its school. To this day I don't remember the name of Corey's pre-school teacher."

This book may seem to focus on the trivia of day-to-day life in the classroom, forming lines and decorating blackboards—but its real goal is providing the foundation for life-changing moments. And because we are indeed teachers, we ask, "What does each step look like?" Welcome to my album.

Sixty-five Things About Planning

Five Things to Do Before the First Day

I love the very beginning of the year. We Jewish teachers are not only looking inward and preparing ourselves spiritually, we are also looking forward and preparing ourselves and our classrooms to meet new faces and new challenges. Here is a short list of things to do before the first day.

1 *Prepare your students and their parents.* Ten days to two weeks before school starts, get your class list. Mail a letter to each student that includes:

[a] welcome

[b] something about yourself

[c] some things to expect on the first day of school and throughout the year

[d] something to bring on the first day of school (an item for a tzedakah project, canned food, something for the mitzvah crib) and

[e] directions for completing a name tag (which has been included in the letter), writing a short autobiography or completing an interest survey.

2 *Prepare your classroom.* Consider the room arrangement. Where will students sit? How will kids know where to sit? Where will students put coats, notes, tzedakah, projects, homework? Where will pencils, paper, textbooks, art supplies be kept for easy access and safe storage? What special problems must be considered if you are sharing a classroom?

3 *Prepare your bulletin boards.* Bulletin boards are fun. But teachers shouldn't spend more time creating bulletin boards than lesson plans. Decide how you can create bulletin boards that are integral to the themes or subjects you will be teaching. Put up a background, perhaps a border. Then include the students in the rest of the planning. If you don't have a bulletin board, create a free-standing kiosk from foam core or pegboard that can be easily folded and stored in a closet.

4 *Prepare for small emergencies—your own and the kids'.* I think it's useful to have a drawer that contains Band-Aids, Kleenex, etc. Be pro-active. We don't want to use precious time or interrupt the flow of a lesson when Josh gets a bloody nose in the middle of Hebrew class.

5 *Prepare for big emergencies.* How are fire drills handled in your school? What is the procedure for getting a substitute? Who on the staff is trained in CPR? First aid? What is your school's policy regarding students who arrive early or are left waiting for a ride home?

Five Things I Wish I Had Done at the Beginning of the Year, or Is It Too Late to Put Up a Time-Line?

Usually about January or February teachers find themselves wishing. I wish I didn't have to collect twenty-five egg cartons for the Tu biShvat project. Or they are thinking, I have a great idea for an end-of-the-year project, but I would have needed to lay the groundwork at the beginning of the year. Here are five things to do now that will help to alleviate the winter "I wish" blues.

1 *Skip lines in the roll book.* The names are easier to read. An extra line leaves room for notes (Bob needs make-up quiz), nicknames, Mrs. Goldberg's new married name.

2 *Write a letter to yourself at Rosh ha-Shanah.* At the beginning of a new school year we all have hopes and dreams for ourselves and our students. Just before school starts set some of these ideas on paper and seal in an envelope. Open and read the letter at the beginning of the second semester. This is a wonderful way to take stock mid-year, to remind yourself of those dreams that you might have lost sight of, and to remember that you were once a kid yourself.

3 *Give parents a list of needed materials and supplies.* This is a great opportunity to acquire the year's supply of egg cartons, tongue depressors, magazines, fabric swatches. Find an appropriate place to store all the materials and they'll be ready for any project you've planned.

4 *Plan an opening activity that can serve as the basis for a year-end project.* This provides an opportunity to demonstrate to the students their growth and progress over the year. A first-day activity might involve writing an autobiography, filling in some completion sentences, a picture of the family (with labels). Repeat the activity at the end of the year. Let the students compare and talk about what has changed since the first day of class.

5 *Create an ongoing project that takes all year to complete.* Examples: [a] if students are learning the alef-bet, you might want to have each child create his/her own alef-bet book, completing a page each week.

[b] Students can make holiday, life cycle, or celebrations books. Collate each child's work, have students make a wonderful cover, and send it home at the end of the year. Older students may create their own Hebrew dictionary, biographies of Torah scholars, or an abbreviation dictionary.

[c] At the beginning of the year create a portfolio for each child. Every two or three weeks ask students to choose a piece of writing or art to keep in the portfolio. At the end of the year ask students to look over and discuss their year's work.

Five Challenges for the Second Day of Class

I do a lot of teacher training workshops. I am usually asked to train brand-new teachers, and I concentrate on getting them ready for the first day—I talk about sending letters home to students and their parents. I've even developed a checklist for the first day of class, so no detail will be left unplanned. I've never thought much about the second day of class. The reality is that day two may be more critical than day one.

On the first day of class the stage is set for teaching and learning. The real challenge comes on day two.

1 *Move beyond first-day routines.* Administrivia looks different. On day one we explain rules, standards, expectations, procedures. We prepare for those students whose names were on the roster and for those whose names weren't on the roster but showed up anyway. On day two every student is expected (with plans for a few who continue to trickle in or who "just moved to town this week"). Students are expected—they have desks, chairs, name cards, mailboxes, places to hang their coat and job assignments. The art project they did the first day is on the bulletin board for them to see when they come in the second day. The daily schedule that you described last time is now on the board. Students know exactly what to do when they walk in the room.

2 *Actualize your first-day observations.* Prove that you listened and paid attention. Demonstrate that you remember everyone's name and something learned about every student. As you stand at the door to greet entering students, make an appropriate personal comment to each one. "You know, Sarah, when I read your biography card I saw that the last book you read was *Beloved*. I read that, too, this summer. I'd love to talk with you about it when things settle down."

3 *Start building community.* On day one we do a lot of "let's get aquatinted and learn each other's names." Now the real community building begins. Design some activities for which students must work together in small groups. Teach them how to work together. Day two is for setting directions for how you're going to work and study together for the entire year.

4 *Build home/school relationships.* You may have sent a letter home before the year started. Now take a few minutes after class to make a quick phone call to each parent—sometimes we call them "one-minute phone calls." "Hello, Mrs. Gamoran. This is Carol Starin, Shauna's teacher at Hebrew High. I just wanted to take a minute to introduce myself and tell you that I'm here for her and for you as she makes the transition into high school. I'm thrilled that Shauna is going to be a *madrikhah* at temple. She made some very astute comments about teaching young children."

5 *Renew the excitement.* Keep every moment fresh. Reinforce the rules, but put your time into planning the content. What am I going to teach? How can I design lessons that capture the imagination and challenge kids to think and grow Jewishly?

Rabbi Nachman of Bratslav said that the biggest sin in the world is doing anything for the second time. How does this thinking apply to the second day of class?

Some good resources: Harry Wong, *The First Days of School: How to Be an Effective Teacher*; Linda Shalaway, *Learning to Teach*; Bonnie Williamson, *A First Year Teacher's Guidebook for Success*.

Five Reasons to Stand by the Door

The classroom is ready. There is a seat for everyone (and a few extras for those who register late). The day's schedule is on the board. Each parent and each student has received a personal letter from you—your first contact in establishing a relationship with students and with parents. The first day is completely planned—in fact, over-planned—because things tend to move more quickly than we think.

You are standing at the door. You will greet each student and welcome him or her. You will be available to each parent who also comes to the door. This is something you will want to continue each and every week.

Teaching is all about relationships—with colleagues, with students, with parents. All the more so in Jewish schools because we are teaching a tradition, a life-style, a Jewish way of thinking and behaving. We want parents to become partners in their child's Jewish education. We want to create a relationship with students that continues beyond the last day of class. Standing at the door for five to ten minutes prior to the beginning of class provides many opportunities to begin and build upon this relationship.

Here are five reasons to stand at the door on the first day and at the beginning of every class session. STANDING AT THE DOOR:

1 *Demonstrates to students that they are expected and welcome* and depicts you as a caring, inviting teacher. Students, especially young ones, have expectations, fears, questions, and uncertainties. Will my teacher like me? What is expected of me? A smiling, welcoming teacher can alleviate some of those fears before the child walks into the classroom.

2 *Provides you with an opportunity to greet each student by name* and to make a personal comment: How is your sister feeling? Did your grandma come home from the hospital? How was the algebra/SAT/driver's test?

3 *Allows you to get a barometer reading on each child.* If you see that a child's eyes are red from crying, a personal comment may turn that around. If you see a child arguing with his parents, you may be able to redirect the conversation. If a child tells you that she had to leave without breakfast, you may decide to serve snack early that day.

4 *Gives you a chance to build a relationship with parents* and/or carpool drivers; to learn that Josh has to leave early for a dental appointment; to invite Sara's family to your home for Shabbat; to find out that Kevin has horrible nightmares; that Bob feels like he has no friends; that Jeff's father is ill; that Jill's parents are getting a divorce; or that Amy has a learning disability. All of these kinds of information help you to know your students and to work with them more effectively.

5 *Gives you an opportunity to direct students to an activity* that they can engage in until class begins. The *"what to do before class begins"* time should be planned for and structured—this is learning time, too. As you greet students, point out some new library books, games or puzzles; a problem, news item or assignment in a specially designated place on the chalk or bulletin board; one of the cases or problems that is discussed weekly in the *Torah Aura Bulletin Board, C. Ha.,* or *Bim Bam.*

Five Things to Do in the First Fifteen Minutes

Last week my friend Maria did a teacher workshop focusing on meeting the needs of different types of learners. Somehow the conversation turned to some of the things that prevent/undermine effective teaching. The most common complaint was not having enough teaching time. Some teachers have as little as two hours of class weekly. Many teachers said there are so many students who straggle in during the first fifteen minutes of class that planning something meaningful is a waste. No matter how much time we have, it is never enough. We need to make the most of every teaching minute—including those first fifteen minutes. The key is to make those first minutes so compelling that students will want to arrive on time. We need to strike a balance: to create activities that are meaningful for the students who are on time. But we don't want to punish the kids who are late because their carpools didn't get them to school on time. You do want to design an activity that motivates the kids to nudge their parents to get them to school on time. You don't want to waste the time of those students who are there when the bell rings. The first fifteen minutes should include activities that enhance the learning experience and are fun, relevant, and challenging. You may also want to make some (or all) of the activities student-directed to free you to talk with students and parents as they arrive.

1 *Develop a selection of games and activities that are completely self-directed* and kept in folders or pockets. For younger students these could include dot-to-dots, simple crossword puzzles, pages cut from workbooks that are no longer in use, or even pictures to color. For older students you might include word of the day, mystery of the day, crack the codes, riddles, book projects, flash cards, or a "challenge of the day" that is always found in the same place (overhead transparency, chalkboard, poster in a corner of the room).

2 *Prepare a journal for each student.* The first few minutes of the day can be designated for journal writing. Motivating questions related to the class curriculum can be put on the overhead projector when students arrive. Use "real life" articles from the newspaper and from *Bim Bam*, cases from *C. Ha*, selections from *Questions Kids Ask*, etc.

3 *Some teachers recommend using the first few minutes for snacks* and/or food preparation. Students may come to class hungry—why wait until mid-morning to feed them? Or plan holiday-related cooking projects. You need to have all supplies ready to use. Braiding a <u>h</u>allah for Shabbat or making *sufganiyot* or *hamantaschen* is a fun activity that not all children get to do at home.

4 *Review prior lessons by using games that kids love.* Jewish Jeopardy can be an ongoing game to which students can continually add questions. Jewish Trivial Pursuit, Hebrew Bingo, Answer to the Question of the day (or week). Offer prizes.

5 *Create a series of learning stations.* Every student chooses one of the learning stations in the room and self-teaches the related activity. Possible learning stations include introduction/review of the lesson, Jewish current events (read news articles and answer questions), *parashat ha-shavuah*, Hebrew word of the day/week/month/year—or any of the above ideas.

Five Things to Include in Your First-Day Plan

It's the first day of class. This day should be carefully planned because it sets the tone for the year. Hopefully you have already made your first contact with students by sending them a letter in the mail. First days need to make students (and parents) feel welcome and comfortable; let them know that you are a dedicated, knowledgeable, prepared teacher and that they will learn a lot.

Plan your first day's schedule to include a get-acquainted activity, a brief discussion about expectations, routines, emergency procedures, and a tour of the building. Effective teaching is nine-tenths planning. Careful planning minimizes management problems and wasted time and gives you a sense of security. When class is ready to begin you need to be standing at the door to greet and welcome students and parents. Do this at the beginning and at the end of EVERY class session. This gives you the opportunity to greet students individually and talk with parents on a regular basis. Make sure your planning includes:

1 *Knowing what the students who arrive early are going to do*

2 *Having a plan for EACH lesson you will teach*

3 *Planning for the transitions BETWEEN lessons*

4 *Setting aside a few minutes at the end of class for closure-summary,* review, some time to motivate and stimulate the lesson for next session

5 *Something for the students to take home*—an art project, newsletter, homework assignment.

Plan for your next step in building the home/school relationship. Within two weeks after the first class, make a one-minute phone call to each parent. Call, introduce yourself, say something positive and personal about their child, tell how and when you can be reached and that you look forward to working with them throughout the year.

Five Things You Should See When You Walk into a Classroom

The room that students walk into should communicate Jewish values in ways that are age-appropriate and relevant to the curriculum. Paying attention to what and how we discard things can prompt a series of Jewish lessons.

1 *A recycle box* is a constant example of one way we can take care of our world. It reflects the mitzvah of *bal tashhit*, no wasting. Another box marked *"geniza"* teaches a different lesson. Jews take special care of sacred books that are discarded. In some schools, photocopies that contain God's name are never destroyed. The *geniza* is the place where they are kept.

2 *Classes should have a Jewish calendar* and age-appropriate related visuals that help kids understand that there are Jewish ways of marking time. Some examples are a moon-watching chart with a prayer for the new month, a way to mark each student's Hebrew and secular birthday, a holiday "train" or some way of visually teaching the cycle of the Jewish year.

3 *Does your class have evidence of an ongoing tzedakah or mitzvah project?* Instead of (or in addition to) passing around the brown envelope every week, why not take on a project? Choose one that grows out of your curriculum. Or check out the suggestions outlined in the ZIV tzedakah report: setting up a mitzvah crib, collecting eyeglasses, dumpster diving, etc. Display artifacts from this process.

4 *Create systems that encourage student independence* and free up the teacher to spend more time with students. Some people call them teacher time-savers. Devise a system by which students can check in when they arrive. Set aside a place to put homework, notes from home, notes to go home. Have an opening activity on the board, overhead, or chart. Be sure the daily plan is posted. If appropriate, have students conduct the opening routines.

5 *On the first day of school each year most classes work together to create a set of rules* or some type of code/commandments to live by. Post the rules so you and the students can refer to them at any time and parents and guests will also know what is expected of everyone who enters the room.

And, of course, put up a *mezuzah* and other appropriate Jewish objects and ritual items as well as pictures, mobiles, student writing and art, or Israel posters. If yours is a Hebrew class or a class where Hebrew is emphasized, label everything and fill the environment with Hebrew books, puzzles, games, music, tapes. In addition, photographs of your class and some of the events of the year are always attention-getters.

Five Things Teachers Should Keep in Their Trunks

One of the wonderful things about teaching is that no two days (no two hours!) are exactly the same. There are always surprises. And there are always moments for which we are not prepared—a lesson that fails, a specialist who doesn't show up, a child who gets hurt at recess, a lesson that takes much less time than planned, a day you wake up with the worst migraine. To begin 1998 we asked five teachers to submit lists of things they keep in their cars. "Be prepared" is not just for Boy Scouts—it's also a must for teachers.

Paul Epstein's list:

1. Koosh ball or flowy scarves
2. Bottle of water
3. Bags or Tupperware
4. Masking tape and scissors
5. Crayola Model Magic (a white clay that dries in twenty-four hours)

Joanne Glosser's list:

1. A great book of stories. Examples: *Does God Have a Big Toe?* by Marc Gellman; a book of Peninnah Schram's stories; *While Standing on One Foot; Puzzle Stories and Wisdom Tales for the Jewish Tradition* by Nina Jaffe and Steve Zeitlin
2. A couple of kippot
3. A Hebrew dictionary
4. Names, addresses, and phone numbers of all students, faculty, and administrators
5. A first-aid kit and some emergency supplies (Kleenex, Band-Aids, safety pins, needle and thread, personal supplies for teenage girls)

Dorothy Glass's list:

1. *The How to Handbook for Jewish Living* (Volumes I and II) by Kerry Olitzsky and Ronald H. Isaacs
2. A box of index cards with questions that cover all subjects learned in class so far
3. Emergency crafts project
4. An emergency stash of compassion
5. A sense of humor

Debbie Findling and her colleagues at the BJE's list:

1. A Tanakh (Bible)

2. Big chocolate bar

3. Change of clothes (shoes, gloves, extra pantyhose)

4. A tape player and Jewish music tapes: a great video (for when you arrive at school with a pounding headache)

5. An earthquake preparedness kit (these folks work in San Francisco)

Amy Azaroff's list:

1. A siddur (prayerbook)

2. Index cards—large white ones and small ones of all colors

3. Permanent markers of all colors and varying thicknesses

4. Alef-bet flash cards

5. Jewish calendar

Five Ways to Create Community in the Classroom

For Jews the concept of "community" is an organizing principle and a philosophy. *Klal Yisrael* is a Jewish value, and it means "we are all responsible for each other." It is expected that caring for and about each other is central to the way we live our lives. How can we teach our children about community? How can a community be created in a class of children who are not neighbors and who may not see each other more than several hours each week?

The "five things advisory group" sent in dozens of suggestions for creating community in the classroom. I have grouped them by category.

1 *"Furniture, furniture, furniture,"* says Paul Epstein. Create a physical environment that encourages students to work collaboratively. Desks, chairs and tables should be arranged to build community. Three or four round tables so students can work independently or in teams work well.

2 *Make students responsible for class life.* Create a "buddy" system so that when a child is absent he/she receives a call from his/her buddy. Keep carbon paper in the class so students can take notes for those who are absent. Develop systems that make the students responsible for class routines: taking attendance; collecting tzedakah; leading *tefillah*, songs, and discussions; preparing, serving, cleaning up the snack.

3 *Get to know parents and students well enough so that you can participate in their community.* Notice important events in students' lives. Celebrate birthdays. Send a note when a parent or sibling is seriously ill or there is a death in the family. Invite the whole class to your home—prepare a meal or holiday food together. Relate to the kids as whole people rather than as students who come in at nine and leave when the final bell rings.

4 *Involve parents.* Invite parents, on a rotating basis, to talk about their jobs. Utilize their skills and energy. You may have parents who are experts in Sephardic/Egyptian cuisine. Invite them to share their expertise. One of the parents in Tina's school is a pediatric oncologist who is very involved with the Tomorrow's Children Fund. That organization has become one of the school's favorite tzedakah projects.

5 *Develop a list of drama, games, activities, and strategies that help students to know each other.* Some examples:

[a] Three truths and a lie. Each person tells three truths and a lie, and the group has to guess which is the lie.

[b] Each week choose one student who is "Student of the Week." That student brings family photographs, a favorite book, game, toy, or family story to share with the class.

[c] Read up on cooperative learning and other group-learning techniques. Use cooperative learning structures. Pair students to discuss and answer questions asked in class. Remember that studying with a partner (_hevruta_) is a traditional Jewish way to learn. Peer teaching is another excellent community-building strategy.

[d] Celebrate class accomplishments: a siddur party or a shiur when the class completes a chapter or unit of study.

[e] Create a class slogan, theme, banner, song.

Building community is about building relationships. We need to begin in our preschools so that when our students take their roles in the adult community they will be living _Klal Yisrael_, the unity of all Jews.

Five Things You Can Do to Energize and Recapture Your Classroom for the Rest of the Year

It's the time of the year when kids are looking out the window. Winter doldrums are over. The sixth graders are beginning to act like seventh graders. March comes in like a lion and goes out like a lamb, but the kids do just the opposite. Begin livening up the classroom by rearranging the furniture, and move on to more substantive ways to recapture your class:

1 *Liven up the classroom by escalating the activity level.* Try new and bigger venues—e.g., the synagogue social hall. Plan structured experiences outdoors: Jewish Jeopardy, Hebrew baseball, Around the World, etc.

2 *Use drama in the classroom.* My colleague, Paul Epstein, shares two ideas. The first is to use the exciting moments that are inherent in the spring holidays as a basis for activities: groggers, plagues, miracles. The second is just one of fifty-one drama activities he shared at a recent mini-CAJE. It's called Timeline: Three or four actors create a scene based on a suggestion from the text. Tell them their scene should be about two minutes long. Once they have created their scene, replay it in one minute. Then in thirty seconds. Then in five seconds. Paul says that this is a great way to review a portion of text and to see what stands out as the most vivid or the most important dramatic detail.

3 *Create a classroom "event."* Plan a program to which you invite families or another class to view or participate in a play, or "sedra-scene," based on an area of your curriculum.

4 *Create a parent program.* A few years ago Joel Grishaver invited parents to class and included text study, an interactive tzedakah piece, a picnic and a parent/student baseball game. His book, *Jewish Parents: A Teacher's Guide,* has dozens of ideas for family education days.

5 *Create a project for your class to leave as a legacy to the school or to next year's class.* Design a wall hanging or quilt to hang. Give each student one large square on which to illustrate a portion of a text or event from the curriculum you are teaching. Find a parent or older student who is willing to sew the patches together and put on a backing and loops for hanging from a pole. A similar project can be done with ceramic tiles; each child creates a tile that is then cemented with all the others and framed to create or decorate a wall in the school. The tiles could also be designed as a table or bench for the synagogue foyer.

It is the time of year when, with less than two weeks to Purim, five weeks to Pesah and twelve weeks to Shavuot, it seems that we have a full plate. But then the sun comes out, and the kids get antsy (and start their own countdown). With some new tricks we can relieve that second-semester angst by keeping the kids motivated and involved.

Five Great Year-End Activities

Plan now for the last day of class. Culminating activities and projects are great opportunities to wrap up the year, review what has been learned, and help kids become aware that meaningful learning has taken place. Each of the following projects should focus on a theme/idea/concept studied during the year.

1 *Design a museum.* Develop a set of criteria and have the class choose "artifacts" for display. Discuss why each was chosen. Write, record, or draw a description. Include facts, stories, and insights about each.

2 *Develop a life-size walk-on board game in which people are the "pieces."* Students create rules and format, as well as "question" and "action" cards.

3 *What would your class want to tell next year's class?* Have them create a video that gives an overview of the class, discussing content and expectations, telling stories and demonstrating examples of what they learned.

4 *Write a class newspaper with news, features, columns, editorials and interviews* that center on a theme or topic studied during the year. Photocopy and send home on the last day.

5 *Create a tzedakah, holiday, mitzvah, parashah, or prayer fair.* This works well on a school-wide basis with each class contributing a display, booth, or interactive station. (Sample activities include games, crafts, letter-writing to Congress, tzedakah box making, a prayer for the *Kotel* [Western Wall].)

Invite the families to participate in your year-end project. Close the day by talking about meaningful Jewish activities to do during the summer. Put a newsletter in their hands and stand together to sing songs such as Debbie Friedman's *L'khi Lakh* or *T'filat ha-Derekh*, wishing everyone a wonderful summer journey.

Five Things to Do on the Last Day of School

It's easy to gather ideas for the first day of school. Every book of teaching ideas has lists, checklists, for how to get ready, for what to do the first day, the first week, the first month. Almost no one talks about the importance of the last day of the school year. The last day is not the time to get the kids to help you take down the bulletin boards and clean out the paste jars. The last day is an opportunity to review what has been learned, to help your students see what they have achieved and accomplished, to provide closure, and to preserve memories.

1 *Create a board game in which students roll dice, move a marker, and choose a card with questions.* For very young children it can be a huge walk-on board game. One week before the end of school the entire class can develop a set of questions as a means of reviewing the year. Questions can be categorized, cards color-coded (e.g., blue holiday questions). More simply, create a list of questions, divide the class in to two teams and play the game. "Winners" get to serve the cake at the closing party.

2 *Create the "Dalet Class Book of Lists."* Use the last two sessions to develop a series of lists: the ten best things we did this year; mitzvot we studied; songs, prayers, stories we learned; boys/girls in the class; teachers in the school; people who work in the synagogue; classmates' autographs (or biographies); what you find in the *Bet K'nesset* (sanctuary); holiday foods; stories we read; bible heroes; funniest things that happened in class. Duplicate and let everyone make a book to take home.

3 *Write a class newspaper.* Brainstorm and list news and feature (cartoons, advice column, recipe, interviews) items; assign one or two articles to each student. Write the articles in pre-designed columns, glue them (if you're not using a computer) onto 11"x17" (which is planned for tabloid-folding) paper, and photocopy for each student to take home.

4 *Leave a legacy for the school.* Create a wall-hanging for the entrance to or foyer of your school or synagogue. Have the students develop a list of things or concepts they studied during the year. Each student chooses a topic to develop and illustrate. Use fabric crayons and transfer each illustration to a 12"x12" square (note: words must be written backwards). A corner square should contain the names of all the kids and the date. Find a student or parent to sew the squares together with a backing and loops for hanging on a pole.

5 *Construct a "Time Capsule."* Ask students to choose one picture or artifact that symbolizes each concept or subject studied during the year. Place everything in a box with a written description (or a riddle) for each. Put the box in a waterproof container and bury it on the school grounds. Leave a map that marks its location.

Your next year's class will have a great time (and an interesting introduction to the year) by digging up the capsule on the first day of school.

Five Things You Can Do to Extend Learning into the Summer

The last day of school shouldn't mark the end of the learning for the year or the end of the relationship you have created with your students. By taking some time now you can continue to teach, inspire and motivate throughout the summer months.

1 *A memory book is what Donna Gordon Blankinship is sending home* with her third graders. Each page will remind students of something they studied during the year with a follow-up/extension activity for each. She's even planning to include a marble from the class "mitzvah marble jar" with suggestions for summertime mitzvah opportunities.

2 *A three-month Jewish calendar of Jewish activities,* games, websites, things to do, places to go and people to see throughout the summer would be a wonderful thing to develop with your colleagues. Include moon watching and Rosh Hodesh activities (the new Jewish month is celebrated through observing the new moon). Add films, television programs, plays, and public park activities that have Jewish content, indicating appropriate calendar dates.

3 *Continue weekly Keren Ami.* You've probably been collecting tzedakah every week. Paul Epstein suggests continuing that activity throughout the summer. Have each student make a tzedakah box (example: a margarine tub that has been attacked by découpage or papier mâché) to take home, with a note explaining how to use it. Ask students to make a weekly contribution—Shabbat is a good time to do this. At the end of the summer children and their families can decide where to send the money. Or (if this is an all-school project) students can bring their tzedakah boxes on the first day of school and empty them into a huge see-through container in the front hall of the school.

4 *Send home a set of activity or game cards that have multiple uses.* You could use the case studies from C. Ha, affixing one case to each card, or a set of "table topics" that grows out of your curriculum. If you have been studying Hebrew letter recognition, send home a pack of letter cards with many ideas for using them (Concentration, Lotto, Bingo, etc.)

5 *Write to your students.* Get addresses of their summer camp and Israel programs as well as the dates they will be attending. Keep the relationships going. Let them know you care about them even when they've moved on to the next grade. Encourage them to write to you (even if they don't go anywhere). Julie Katz suggests giving each student a stamped postcard. Ask students to write your address and, at some time during the summer, write you and tell you what they're doing.

And for good measure: Rabbi Aryeh Blaut gives his students an opportunity to study all the summer parashot (Torah portions). Each student takes home a packet of daily parashah activities (parent signatures were required). Last summer Eliezer Kletenik (age nine) even took his activity packet to camp.

Forty-five Things About School-to-Home Communications

Five Reasons to Send a Letter Home at the Beginning of the Year

You can begin building a positive relationship with your class and their families even before school begins. Get your class registration list. Ten days to two weeks before school starts send a letter to each student and, possibly, also to each family. Computers make it easy to personalize each letter and to write in a large font for K's and 1's. For some children this will be the first personally addressed letter they will ever receive.

Here are five reasons to send this letter to students:

1 *It's "money in the bank."* You can read about "money in the bank" in Joel Lurie Grishaver and Ron Wolfson's book, *Jewish Parents: A Teacher's Guide.* "Money in the bank" is what we talk about when we say "I owe you one." Kids feel like they "owe us one" when they believe that we know and care about them. The letter home begins this process.

2 *It tells parents and students that you are confident and well organized.*

3 *It provides an opportunity for you to talk about your background,* philosophy and plans for the year.

4 *It makes kids feel expected and welcome.*

5 *It can set up a first-day activity or event.*

Five things to include in the letter:

1 *A welcome*

2 *Something about yourself*

3 *Some things to expect on the first day of school and throughout the year*

4 *Something to bring on the first day of school* (an item for a tzedakah project, canned food, something for the mitzvah crib)

5 *Directions for completing a name tag* (which has been included in the letter), writing a short autobiography or completing an interest survey.

Note: There will always be students who don't receive your letter because they register on the first day of school. Have extras of everything so they feel welcome, too.

Five Tips for Effective Parent-Teacher Conferences

Parent-teacher conferences, "open house," and curriculum night are links in the chain of parent/school communication that, ideally, began even before school started, with a letter home. Newsletters, participation in family learning events, and family homework also maintain an ongoing relationship and insure that parents know what's happening in class. Our relationships with our students and their families extend beyond the classroom at many levels. We see our students and their parents at shul, at bar/bat mitzvah parties, at lectures, at community fundraisers. Our social and religious contacts will be much more comfortable if our professional contacts are positive, are supportive, and grow out of mutual respect. The purpose of the parent-teacher conference is to get and give information and to find solutions to problems.

1 *Before phoning to schedule a conference, write down what you want to say.* If there is a problem, state it in terms of concern for the student. Decide who needs to be involved in the conference. Sometimes it is very beneficial to invite the student to come with his/her parents. You may want to rehearse or role-play with another teacher or with your administrator.

2 *Be sure parents know what your goals are for their child,* what you are doing to achieve your goals and how their child is moving toward those goals.

3 *Find out what the parents want to know.* Too often parents come away from a conference without knowing any specifics. They want to know more than the fact that Sarah gets along well with the other kids or that you really enjoy having her in class. They need to know what Sarah is learning and to see examples of her work.

4 *Be a good listener.* Ask parents to tell you about their child's interests, habits, responsibilities. Be alert to information that will give you insights into the child and the family situation.

5 *If there is a problem, this shouldn't be the first time parents are hearing about it.* There should be no surprises. Discuss problems in terms of finding solutions. How can the parents help at home? How can you help at school? Make sure you let parents share their take on the classroom situation and what may improve it. Be an active listener and show parents that you have heard their insights. Most parents will listen to you only after you have proved that you are listening to them.

Begin the conference positively. Keep in front of you a checklist of topics you want to discuss. End the conference with the next step in place. When will you talk next? When is the next family education day? The next newsletter? What is the next link in the chain? Encourage the parents to contact you personally if they think of other important items that may help you as their child's teacher.

Five Key Points to Keep in Mind when Writing Progress Reports and Five Tips about Progress Reports

"Technically your grade is incomplete—but…" With that comment Joel begins a wonderful, thoughtful comment on Avi's report card—insights that are built upon a real relationship with Avi (*Jewish Parents: A Teacher's Guide,* p. 108).

It happens every year. Sometimes twice. The principal announces that it's time to send home reports to parents. Usually the format is predetermined. Whether they are called report cards or progress reports, whether they follow or precede parent conferences (or not), whether you like the format or not, it is the teacher's job to fill it out and send it home.

1 *The progress report is another piece of the home-school relationship.* Hopefully this progress report will not be the first time a parent has heard from you. Problems need to be addressed as they occur.

2 *Personal comments are critical.* If the form you are required to use does not have a place for comments, create an insert that allows you to write a narrative.

3 *Comments not only tell something about the student,* they tell something about you. Use appropriate grammar, spelling and sentence structure.

4 *Parents and kids want to receive meaningful information* that communicates two messages: You actually know the child because you have a relationship with the him/her; you can describe how the student is doing in each area of the curriculum. Work habits, core values, interpersonal skills need to be addressed, too.

5 *Include a curricular outline or list of class goals and objectives* so parents will have a context for your comments.

Five Tips about Progress Reports

1 *Provide a summary using plain language.*

2 *Choose the most appropriate issues to address.*

3 *Be balanced.* Praise the strengths (every child has them) and be constructive (not obtuse) in areas that need improvement.

4. *Be descriptive.* Tell what the student has done. This is not the place to make major interpretations or suggest major interventions.

5. *Be careful about words like "should" and "must."*

Report Cards: Five Tips for Writing Meaningful Comments

"Craig needs to take a more serious interest in our class activities. He knows his prayers well but needs to participate more actively."

I wrote that in 1966. Craig was a first grader in my class. Looking back, I'm lucky that Craig's parents didn't sue me for incompetence.

In Jewish schools it's important that the report card (or progress report) serve as an integral part of the school-home relationship. Concerns about students should be communicated in person or by phone. Even parents whose children are doing well want more information. All of our home-school communications should contribute to the partnership we are building.

If you do have to write progress reports, make them as meaningful as possible. Parents want to be informed.

With the progress report should come a detailed letter of skills, content, concepts and learning experiences of the grading period so that parents know what has been evaluated. It's helpful for parents to know what the teacher has used for evaluation purposes: written tests, collaborative group projects, one-on-one assessments of reading fluency and comprehension, etc.

Here are some examples:

1 *Morah Michal used to write this comment to her Kitah Gimel* (5th grade) students: "Rachel, you've made great strides this term in ——, and I encourage you to be proud of your accomplishments."

But more importantly, Michal discussed the comments with each student before sending them home. This strategy ensures that kids see their own reports and have a chance to react. Michal always asked her students to set a goal for the next term, with her input, and then she included that goal in her own comments.

2 *Josh has mastered the skills of* _____ and has demonstrated a remarkable grasp of the concepts _____ as reflected in his project/paper on _____.

3 *Not only is Marsha an exceptional student,* she is also a mentsch who _____ (describe an example of her mentschlich behavior.) Next semester I'd like to see her work toward the goal of _____ (it can be an academic goal like mastering the next set of prayers or learning Torah trope, or it can be a behavioral goal like increasing her confidence in taking risks to make a mistake without being so hard on herself).

4. *This next example is one in which the message is ambiguous* because the language carefully couches the real meaning.

"Sarah is an independent thinker. She often brings in many associations between her life experience and classroom learning. Her eagerness to share often leads to a valuable contribution. Sarah seems to be using this year to learn more about becoming part of a group. Her love of Judaism leads the class to new tunes for prayers and new ways of making connections."

Sarah's parents probably won't see through the nice words to the tachlis. Be kind, but clear: "Sarah's eagerness to share is commendable, but her comments are not always on subject. We need to help Sarah _____."

5. *Shoshana is really blossoming.* This term I have seen her move from _____ to _____. I was impressed by Shoshana's comprehension of our tzedakah lesson when she brought her tzedakah games from home.

What goes around, comes around. (That squirmy disinterested Craig became the editor of our local Jewish newspaper. There are now times when I have to beg him to write articles about my projects.)

Five Ways to Enlist Parents to Help in the Classroom

Involving parents is a key way to help build personal relationships as well as the home-school partnership. Parent-teacher collaboration benefits the kids, the teacher, and the school. Parents can be resources to enhance your program. Parents can use their connections and networks to link you to the wider community.

1 *Use the language of invitation.* Linda Kirsch recommends personal phone calls. Even if parents sign the "volunteer form" to be class parents, they need a personal touch. Encourage teachers to call parents and talk to a human, not a machine, when asking for help with special projects or classroom activities.

2 *Ask parents for specific kinds of help.* Call two or three weeks in advance. "We're going to create a tzedakah quilt and really need some extra hands." Debi Rowe has found that even if parents have a scheduling conflict, they will usually ask for a rain check—and follow through. Idie Benjamin uses a lot of contraptions in her classroom She asks handy parents to help build the sukkah and the huge outdoor menorah.

3 *Adapt the "Appleseed" project.* The Petroff children go to a public school where parents are asked to help "seed" their children and the school community by committing to a variety of activities. They can be active in helping their own children learn (reading together, helping with homework, etc.), and they volunteer to help the school community by making phone calls, tutoring, helping in class, being a reading buddy. Every parent who signs a pledge to take this on is recognized on a large apple tree display, with family names on the paper apples. Iris suggests a Jewish adaptation by asking parents to listen to a child practice Hebrew reading, share a favorite Jewish story, coordinate a schoolwide special event.

4 *Create a parent interest form.* Many schools do this at the beginning—or even before the beginning—of the school year. Some schools integrate the parent interest form right into the registration process. Ask parents to write down their skills and areas of interest, hobbies, collections, etc. You will know just who to call for tutoring, storytelling, drama, music, library, Internet, nature/science, art, craft projects.

5 *Use e-mail effectively.* Many '90s parents disregard all paper mail but read their e-mail because it's more concise and interactive. Create and maintain a list of parents' e-dresses and send updates of school and classroom programs and activities.

Cautions

1 *Working with parents adds to a teacher's work.*

2 *Once we ask for their commitment, we must provide the tools needed to be successful.*

3 *Don't assume parents will know what to do.* Their tasks will need to be pre-planned and explained.

4 *If we ask for their help, we must use it.*

5 *Parents must be appropriately thanked and recognized.*

When Children Have Two Homes

When I was growing up in the fifties I didn't know anybody whose parents were divorced. On the surface it looked like all my temple friends had "Leave it to Beaver" families and lives. Today when you read the list of consecration students in the synagogue newsletter it is commonplace to see children who are listed as son of Harry Goldberg and Rena Goldberg.

In these days of joint custody arrangements it is not uncommon to find students in our classes who spend part of the week with their mother and part of the week with their father or who alternate weekends. Here are five strategies for working with children who have two homes.

1 *Get to know both parents.* It is very important to assure parents that you want to work with them so that their child will have a successful Jewish school experience. Learn about the custodial arrangements, carpool arrangements, and how the parents want the school to handle mail—flyers, announcements, report cards, homework. (The school should set up all forms to be sensitive to these issues.) The parents may be looking to you for help.

2 *Set up systems.* Just as many of these kids have two sets of clothes—one in each home—they may need to be provided with two sets of textbooks—one set in each home. I have talked with some teachers who keep a set of textbooks in the classroom, always available for children who forget or didn't come from the home where the books and materials are kept.

3 *Watch your language!* Don't envision a Shabbat table where Mother lights the candles, Father makes kiddush and Ward and June bless the kids. Be sensitive when you talk about parents and families, holidays and rituals. Try, "If your mother or your father..." When talking about homes, interchange "house" and "apartment."

4 *Develop strategies that create community in the classroom.* Use group and cooperative activities so kids can get to know each other by working together. Create a classroom where the kids know what to expect. Kids of divorced parents have lives that have been ripped apart. We must create a classroom that is safe and comfortable. Develop routines and procedures that kids can kids can count on—a smiling, caring face and opening activities that children can look forward to. Be sensitive to children who might have stressful lives, children who might be in crisis.

5 *Celebrate the diversity of family life in your curriculum.* When possible, create lessons that may have special messages for these kids—e.g., a lesson on sacred space that validates all types of living situations.

Issues related to divorce are complicated and greatly affect the children—our students. Custodial arrangements, financial arrangements, remarriage (remarriage to a non-Jew) must come into play when we work with these kids and with their families. Here we talked about ways to help the child who has two Jewish parents in a custodial arrangement where the child is shuttled between two homes. In the next chapter we'll talk about ways that we, as teachers and principals, can work with families where the situation is complicated by other factors, such as remarriage to a non-Jew.

When Children Have Two Homes II: Dealing with Two Families

"I am faced this year with a student who is caught in a custody battle between a Jewish and a non-Jewish parent. She will be joining my third grade class every other Sunday so that she can also attend Sunday school at church."

"There's a child in my class whose parents divorced last year. Dad remained in our synagogue. Mother joined another synagogue. Mom wants Serena to alternate Hebrew schools on the weekends."

"Mr. Goldstein wouldn't let his son go to camp this summer because the camp session infringed on 'his days' with Josh."

These are some of the stories I received in response to previous chapter. Because the subject generated so much conversation, over the next few weeks we're going to build on some of the issues we raised.

1 *Know that there are some battles we can't win.* Most of the difficult issues are about power, control and time—they are not about the child. However, it is the child who often becomes the pawn, the child who is caught in the middle. The situation for "the child" in each of our three cases is less than desirable. Our job is to find ways to not make it worse.

2 *There are some issues that should not be the teacher's problem*—they are the responsibility of the principal, the rabbi and the school board. Admitting a child who will be receiving a dual-faith education is against the policy of all of the major movements and is usually undertaken only in very special circumstances. A whole "plan" as to how to support the child must be developed before such a situation can be managed. Sometimes teachers need permission to not solve the problem.

3 *Sometimes the rabbi must play a central role.* It is the rabbi who must counsel the parent or parents who wanted to alternate between Jewish school and church schools, or even between two Jewish schools. She must help parents see that the situation is untenable and that a choice should be made. It should be one rabbi who calls the other to collectively work with the parents to find the best Jewish choice for Serena. The rabbi should be involved from the moment you learn about one of these difficult situations. The rabbi knows his congregants and must help parents understand what is best for the child.

4 *Now let's talk about the camp problem.* My friend Harlene Appelman thinks that in divorce situations there should be an exemption on all things Jewish; they should not be used as bargaining chips. Jewish schooling, Jewish camping, youth groups, Israel trips, etc. should not be up for negotiation regarding time or money. This is a message we should try to communicate to our parents. Jewish camp should not come out of anyone's days.

5 *Remember, the good of the child is always the goal.* The teacher is the child's advocate. And there are limits to what one can accomplish in class.

When a Child Has Two Homes III: Five Technical Issues

Last week I picked up my copy of our synagogue's new congregational roster. It's really useful because there are pictures of each family. For the first time I noticed something I had never noticed before. There were several instances in which children were photographed with one parent and, further on, photographed with the other parent. Two caring parents. Two families. Two homes.

A NOTE TO PRINCIPALS: When it comes to working with children who have two homes, the principal needs to take the lead. Hopefully you are the type of principal who meets with every new family that comes into your school. That's the time you will find out if there is a separation or divorce, and you can talk about and clarify some of these things before the child even begins school. Otherwise, make the initial contact by phone and clarify some of the custodial and legal arrangements. Each family has a different story. You need to know the stories and give your teacher that information needed to work sensitively with the child and the family.

The principal of a Jewish day school told me about a father who was offended by school forms that used the term "non-custodial parent."

It is the responsibility of the principal to create school registration forms that validate both parents. Instead of spaces for custodial/non-custodial parent, leave spaces for information about mother and father. a) Mother's Name/Address/Phone. b) Father's Name/Address/Phone (if different). c). Child lives with: Mother, Father, both (specify).

Debbie Findling suggests politically correct forms: a) Parent Name/Address/Phone. b) Second Parent Name/Address/Phone. c) Child lives with: Parent _____, Parent _____, Both (specify). This language avoids distinctions and stereotypes and works well for students who have parents of the same sex.

1 *Be pro-active.* Call both parents. Introduce yourself and talk with each of them to clarify information for emergency/medical forms, permission slips, and other forms that may have legal implications. Probably you will want to send most mail—flyers, report cards, etc.—to both homes. Work with the parents to set up a system by which you mail flyers, bulletins, and report cards to both parents. That way you ensure that parents get all the communication and you are not relying on the kids to be the messengers. Don't put the kids in the middle by relying on them to deliver the school's mail.

2 *Information for the public.* When it comes to confirmation, consecration and other kinds of lists that are published in the synagogue newsletter or local Jewish news, talk with the parents about how they want their names listed. When it comes to class rosters that are sent to every family, check with both parents. Sue Littauer makes a good point. She says it's very important to be sure that addresses and phone numbers of both parents are listed to insure that a child is not left off an invitation list and that friends can call to arrange play dates, sleepovers, car pools, youth group meetings and soccer games.

3. *Textbooks and Homework.* "I didn't do my homework because I left my book at my mom's." Some of these kids have enough things to worry about just keeping their schedules straight as to which parent's house they are supposed to sleep at on the second Tuesday of the month. Teachers can help by providing two sets of materials so that one set can be kept at each parent's home. My friend and colleague Joanne Glosser (who is a religious school principal) makes an important point. She says, "Don't charge extra fees for the extra materials or books. Let the school budget swallow it."

Some teachers keep an extra set of books and extra copies of homework in the classroom at all times. Kids with two homes (and kids who are just forgetful) always have what they need to complete their assignments during class times.

4. *Parent conferences and family education days.* Start off the year by asking each of the parents how they would like to be involved. Would they like joint or separate parent conferences? Would they both like to join in at family education programs—or perhaps alternate? In other words, find out what is working best for their family and how you can best meet their needs and keep them involved as you work with their child. Judy Miller, a day school teacher, has conferences with each parent and keeps ACCURATE notes. She sends home a weekly newsletter and mails a copy to the non-custodial parent. She calls BOTH parents to make sure they know about special projects and performances.

5. *Gifts, art projects.* Making a _hannukiyah_ or a kiddish cup or a mezuzah can raise the anxiety level of a child who has two homes. Do I give the ceramic candlesticks to my dad or to my mom? You know if you have students in this situation. You should know their schedules. Armed with that information you can plan projects that minimize the anxiety. You can provide enough materials and manipulate the timing so students can make two. Always tell the child that he/she is welcome to make one project for each parent if desired.

Our job in Jewish schools is to find ways to work with both families in order to minimize the problems and anxieties for the kids, our students. The operative principles are respect, communication, validation, and sensitivity.

A Death in the Family: Five Questions for When Your Student Loses a Family Member

Each child talked about what they remembered about Mia, what they liked about her, what experiences they had together. I had a clear glass of water on the desk as we spoke. When everyone had finished sharing I added a spoonful of sugar to the glass and stirred it. Although the water looked the same, we knew that it was sweeter. Although our lives continue without our friend, they are sweeter for having known her (Faye Tillis Lewy).

Last week two members of my synagogue died. Zach had already told his fellow fourth graders that his father wasn't going to get better. Anya, a ninth grader, had hoped her mother would live until Anya graduated from high school. I saw sixth grade girls help Orly bury her father by shoveling dirt on his coffin. I saw kids and teachers from Hebrew High come with homemade cakes to Anya's home for *shiva minyanim* (memorial services). My own sons were pallbearers at one of the funerals.

Death is part of life. Talking and teaching about death, dying, and mourning is usually (except when we teach "life cycle") not part of our curriculum. It's not a subject that's comfortable—it's a subject many try to avoid. When a student loses a parent or sibling we must find ways—Jewish ways—to talk, write, and read about what's going on. We must be a support to the student and to the classmates who may be wondering if their parents will die, too.

1 *How do you explain things that are unexplainable?* One way is to use books as springboards for discussion.

Bubbe, Me and Memories by Barbara Pomerantz, *Pearl's Marigolds for Grandpa* by Jane Breskin Zalden, *It Must Hurt a Lot: A Child's Book About Death* by Doris Sanford, *Daddy's Chair* by Sandy Lanton, *The Fall of Freddie the Leaf* by Leo Buscaglia. Faye recommends Peninnah Schram's story "Elijah's Mysterious Ways" from *Tales of Elijah the Prophet*, which is also available as a Torah Aura Instant Lesson.

2 *How do you move from a class of kids to a caring community?* Judaism has so many wonderful built-in traditions that enable us to grieve in meaningful ways. Teach students about *kri'ah* (tearing a ribbon or a piece of clothing)—tell them why Becky will be wearing a sweater with a tear. Teach children why we sit shiva (seven days of mourning). Take some students to the funeral and/or to the shiva house. Gather some students together to bake something to take to the family. Teach students that it's important to share stories, to talk about what that person meant to you or your family, how he or she touched your life. Teach students that people live on through the stories we tell. Organize a service at school. Teach appropriate prayers; create a minyan at school.

3 *What kinds of class projects or activities may be appropriate?* Find out what kinds of tzedakah activities/causes the person was interested in. Collect tzedakah and have the class write a letter explaining that the donation is in memory of Becky's sister. One way of helping a person's memory live on is by continuing the work she was doing.

Collect money from the class. Take a few children to a local nursery to pick out a young tree. Gather the entire class to plant the tree in the school garden or courtyard in memory of Joel's brother—a living tribute. Over the years the tree will grow and flourish. Kids can take turns tending the tree—or the whole garden.

Make a class card, with brief messages, signed by every student and sent or delivered to the shiva home.

Writer Rosemary Zibart believes that "writing gives children a voice and validates their feelings." Look for writing opportunities. Create a class book. Students who knew David's mother can share memories or tell stories. Other students create the cover and bind the book.

Torah Aura has other instant lessons that deal with death. These lessons are rich in content and will provide a focus for discussion with older kids. *The Red in My Father's Beard* for grades four to eight deals with traditional Jewish death, burial and mourning rituals; *Remember Me,* for grades six–adult, focuses on the deeds and ideas by which we want others to remember us. The lesson *Pebbles on a Stone* deals with a visit to the cemetery and the unveiling of a tombstone.

4 *How can I "be there" for the student and the family?* You can never know for sure. But you can do some homework. Learn about the family. What kinds of decisions have been made? If the family is doing *kriah,* shiva, *shloshim,* explain each of these rituals to the class. If you are unfamiliar with these rituals, pick up a copy of Ron Wolfson's book (see #5). Visit the student before she comes back to class. Remember that Becky's pain and loss will be with her—and with her family—far past the shiva. Can the school help out by arranging carpools? Babysitters? Be available to listen. Let students have their questions and their fears and tears. "Don't ask and don't feel" is what leads to problems.

5 *What can you do if death is a subject you're not comfortable with or too close to?* Ask for help. Look to your principal. She may want to come into the classroom to facilitate a discussion. Look to your school psychologist—or invite in a community psychologist. Look to your rabbi. Rabbis deal with death and dying all the time. Rabbi David Fine told me that most people are uncomfortable talking about death—especially when talking to a child. "It's like having a white elephant in the class. You can feel it. It's palpable. Everyone knows it's there. But no one talks about it."

Read. There are many fine Jewish books that deal with death, dying, mourning and comforting. I recommend *A Time to Mourn, A Time to Comfort* by Dr. Ron Wolfson. Every chapter contains information about rituals as well as stories, told by people of all ages who have experienced loss. In *The Jewish Teacher's Handbook, Volume III* (A.R.E.), chapter 9, "Teaching About Death and Dying," includes a section that outlines attitudes toward death at different developmental stages.

Fifty-six Things About Lesson Planning

Five Thoughts About Lesson Planning

If you're taking a car trip, the AAA will prepare a Trip-tik. You provide the basic information—point of departure, destination, approximate travel time, some of the sights you'd like to see along the way. They will create for you a book that contains a suggested route with lists of sights, restaurants, hotels—a guidebook designed to meet your specific criteria. A lesson plan is like a Trip-tik. It serves as a guide, helps organize your ideas and provides you with a sense of security. A carefully thought-out plan will keep you from getting lost, prevent time-wasting, and insure that you arrive at your destination.

1 *Knowing your destination is the first step.* What is it that I want my students to know or be able to do by the end of this lesson? This becomes the objective— the destination. All the other lesson components need to help reach that destination. Some examples of objectives: (By the end of the lesson, students will be able to) describe the 4 step *t'shuvah* process; discuss the significance of the sukkah; discuss the lulav and etrog as a metaphor for study and mitzvah; describe home and synagogue rituals associated with Rosh ha-Shanah.

2 *How will I begin the trip in a way that motivates the students and brings them right into the lesson?* This is the set induction. Examples: How is the parsley we dip on Pesa<u>h</u> like the little hot dogs or meatballs we eat before a meal at other kinds of celebrations? How is the Torah like a library? How is Rosh ha-Shanah like the first day of school?

3 *What will I do to convey the concepts and ideas outlined in my objective?* Examples: read a story; show a film; read and discuss a text.

4 *What will my students do that will help them learn and understand what is being taught?* Examples: write a poem, a *d'rash* (a Torah interpretation), a puppet play; create a game, a chart, a drawing, a model; participate in a debate; draw a diagram; or study <u>h</u>evruta style (working in dyads).

5 *Every lesson needs to have a planned closure, a drawing together of the lesson.* Closure is more than just a planned ending. Take a few moments to help students review, to analyze all of the lesson's elements, to make sense of the lesson, to reinforce what has just been learned, to motivate subsequent lessons.

Two final thoughts: First, list all of the materials and resources needed for the lesson. Make sure everything is readily available. Second, after the students leave, perhaps much later in the day, take a few minutes to reflect about your day. What went well? What will I do differently next time? Which students seem to be struggling? Which parents can I call to say "Just want you to know that Josh contributed some great ideas to our discussion about *t'shuvah*."

Five Ways To Begin a Lesson

Get out your homework. We're going to go over the questions you answered at home. Boring...

In teacher jargon we call it a set induction—it's the way a lesson begins. Set inductions are as old as the Talmud. Rabbah used to say something humorous to his scholars before he began teaching, in order to amuse them (*Pesahim* 117a). Even in Talmudic times good teachers knew that they needed to get students' attention and make them feel comfortable.

A good set induction begins the lesson in an involving way. It gets students' attention, recalls prior knowledge, capitalizes on something they already know, zooms them right into the content, and mentally prepares them to learn.

There are all kinds of activities that can serve as great set inductions. Here are five very different examples.

1 *It was a lesson about lost objects.* But the students didn't know that. It was their first Mishnah lesson, but they didn't know that either. As the class came in from recess and hung their jackets in the coatroom, someone spotted some money lying on the floor. Students asked each other, "Do you know who dropped this?" "Finders/keepers!" "What should we do with it?" They were still asking questions when they came in and took their seats and Rivy Kletenik began her first lesson from the Mishnah on damages.

2 *On the first day of the new quarter at the University of Washington,* students entered their Ed. Psych. class and took their seats as the "teacher" took his place in the front and began asking questions. These were really difficult questions, questions students couldn't answer because they had no background, questions that raised their anxiety level. When everyone was very uncomfortable the man at the desk took a seat in the class, and professor Sam Wineburg got up from his seat in the class, put down his backpack, put on his tie and took his place in the front. These students experienced how it felt to be anxious about not knowing the material, afraid to raise their hands, embarrassed in front of their peers, not yet ready to learn.

3 *Shoshana teaches a Hebrew High class about Shabbat.* Every week when the students enter the room they find a beautifully set Shabbat table with Shabbat music playing in the background. The table, music, and ritual items set the tone for each week's instruction.

4 *When she begins her Pesah unit* Eliza M. uses a brainstorming process from *Activators** by Jon Saphier and Mary Ann Haley. She puts three columns on a chart: Know/Think I Know/Want to Know. The entire class brainstorms lots of ideas for each column. Following the brainstorming process students discuss/debate the ideas and their placement. The Know/Think I Know/Want to Know charts are hung in the room and referred to throughout the unit. Saphier suggests that these charts can be put away until the end of the unit, then brought out so students can check the list against what they learned.

5 *Rabbi Aryeh Blaut gives every lesson a catchy title.* Some examples from his Mishnah classes on Berakhot: "oops" (if one has made a mistake), "eeny, meeny, miny, mo" (if many varieties of food were placed before him, and he wants to eat of each kind), "Last, but not least" (which blessings are recited after eating some of the seven species). Students, who are used to looking for the new lesson title on the board, start asking questions as soon as they walk in the room.

More ways to begin a lesson in an involving way: Bring in a prop, a guest, or video. Wear a costume, use a puppet, have the class make/build something according to instructions without knowing what they're building. Other ideas: Demonstrate an experiment, recreate a game show.

*A fabulous resource: *Activators: Activity Structures to Engage Students' Thinking Before Instruction* by Jon Saphier and Mary Ann Haley.

Great Beginnings: Five Objectives—Five Set Inductions

After reading today's column teachers will be able to define and give examples of objectives and set inductions. That's an example of a behavioral objective.

"What are some of the things you do to get ready for the first day of school? What are some of the things you think about the night before the first day of a new school year? We do and feel some of these same things when we begin a new Jewish year." That's a set induction.

The objective provides the underpinning of every lesson. But it's the most difficult part of planning. Once a carefully thought-out objective has been articulated, each subsequent step should fall into place. Begin by asking yourself "What do I want my students to learn or know or be able to do by the end of this lesson?"

The next step is deciding how to begin the lesson. People use different terms: set induction, motivator, anticipatory set, activator. I like set induction. A set induction grabs the students' attention, pulls them into the lesson by relating what will be studied to something with which they are familiar.

Here are five and five.

1 *Objective:* After class discussion, reading lesson two in the Alef curriculum, a visit to the sanctuary, and learning Danny and Jeff's song, students will be able to list the three names for the synagogue and give examples of each.

Set induction: Take the students on a tour of the synagogue. After returning to the classroom ask them to list all the things they see happening. Try grouping the list according to function.

2 *Objective:* Following an experiential exercise, reading a mishnah on damages, and discussion, students will be able to list four considerations when finding a lost item.

Set induction: (In a story we have told before) my colleague Rivy Kletenik taught this lesson by "planting" money in the coatroom that the kids found when they came in from recess. By the time they reached their seats they had already asked the key questions: To whom does this belong? Can I keep it? What if we can't find out who lost it?

3 *Objective:* After reading the text (pages 28-32, *BJL Shabbat*) and examining and talking about the ritual items, students will be able to name the items and tell how each is used for havdalah.

Set induction: Show a havdalah candle, kiddush cup and spice box. Let students touch and smell, then say, "Let's take a look at how we use these things to help us say goodbye to Shabbat."

4 Rabbi Phil Warmflash wrote a wonderful plan for an Instant Lesson called *Remember Me.*

Objective: Students will be able to describe some of the Jewish traditions and values related to memory; to describe and write an ethical will; and to talk about some of the challenges involved in writing an ethical will.

Set induction: A guided fantasy. Students are asked to close their eyes, relax, and imagine they are going to be parents.

5 *Objective:* Following discussion, examples and a story, students will be able to demonstrate, by role playing, writing a puppet play or drawing, that saying "I'm sorry" is the first part of *t'shuvah* (repentence).

Set induction: (A teacher-created scenario) "Josh and Ali stole a candy bar from the store. Josh told his mother that it was Ali's fault, and she got into a lot of trouble from her parents. But Josh didn't get in any trouble. Josh really felt bad. What should he do?" Ask the students to whisper their solutions to their neighbors. Then ask class members to share their solutions.

A great resource: *Activators: Activity Structures to Engage Students' Thinking Before Instruction* by Jon Saphier and Mary Ann Haley.

Five Great Ways to End a Lesson

"Time's up. Put away your books. Let's get ready for Hebrew."

We have so much to teach and so little time that sometimes our lessons run together. Last week we talked about ways to begin a lesson. We focus a lot on beginnings. But there seems to be much less concentration on planning for the end of a lesson. Both are important. "What we do immediately before and immediately after a formal learning experience may matter as much as the learning experience itself" (*Summarizers*, p. ix).

Planning for teaching must include planning for the conclusion of each lesson. Conclusions provide opportunities to draw pieces of the lesson together, give kids a sense of accomplishment, set the stage for or motivate the next lesson, review key points, evaluate the learning, apply the new learning in new ways.

Here are five strategies to get students actively engaged in understanding what they have learned.

1 *The newsletter.* Newsletters can be used very successfully as a concluding activity for an individual lesson, a unit, or at the end of the school day. Written by the class, the newsletter is one page with four boxes. The class decides which activities from the day will be highlighted. The class members contribute to the "articles" (short summaries of the activities). Allowing for creativity, the summaries could be illustrations or poetry as well as prose. Then each student fills in the page and takes it home. Alternately, one student can do the writing and the newsletter can be photocopied for the class to take home.

2 *Digestion questions.* Rabbi Aryeh Blaut ends his lessons with "cliffhangers." He calls them digestion questions—DQs—since it's the last thing students do, like a dessert. The questions are written on the board at the beginning of class and repeated at the end of class. Students attempt to write answers to the DQs. The DQs are collected; some are read aloud. Example questions: "Who sold Yosef to whom? What will become of Yosef? If Reuven really wanted to save Yosef, why didn't he stop the sale? What will Ya'akov think? All this and more in our next exciting Humash (Bible) lesson."

3 *Ticket out the door.* I frequently conclude lessons (and adult workshops) by handing each student a 3"x5" card. I ask them to "Write five adjectives that tell how you felt about this lesson." Or "Write three things you learned about Shabbat candles." Or "Write four words that come from the shoresh ___." "Write one reason why___." Stand by the door. Students put their names on the "ticket" and hand it to you as they leave for recess or at the end of the day. (Doubles as a great attendance-taker.)

4 *Question cards.* Give each student two or three cards. On each card students write one question about an important aspect of the lesson. Collect the cards and pose the questions to the class. Do this activity periodically. Keep all the cards (in a big glass jar), pulling them out for review at the end of a unit, for a meaningful transition time activity, or to use as the question cards with a board game.

5 *3 –2–1* (from *Summarizers*, page 58). The 3-2-1 summarizer is used at the end of a class, reading, movie, etc. Students are asked to write down three things that really interested them; two things they'd like to know more about; and one idea that theywill write about tonight. The headings can be changed to suit the activity.

Bonus ideas:

Quickies: Create a midrash on the material just covered. Ask students to create their own mishnah based on what they have learned about how the mishnah works. Ask students to summarize what they learned by writing a play, song, or rap. Create a game show that reviews the material. Make a generic board game that has question cards with content that grows out of the lesson.

When we conclude the reading of the Torah we say *hazak, hazak, v'nithazek.* It means "Be strong, be strong, and let us be strengthened together." As with the ending of the Torah, we need to end every lesson on a note of strength.

The resource I used for this column was Jon Saphier and Mary Ann Haley, *Summarizers: Activity Structures to Support Integration and Retention of New Learning.*

Transitions: Opportunities—Not Wasted Time

Teacher, I'm done with my work, now what should I do? Some people call it "dead time." For students it's often wasted time. Here are five times during the day when an effective teacher can make the most of those minutes and plan for learning to happen (which also has the benefit of minimizing behavior problems):

a. Students begin to wander into class five to fifteen minutes before the bell rings.

b. Students finish their work early and ask, "What should I do now?"

c. There may be several three- to five-minute periods during a class session when students are between lessons or waiting for the next thing: the arts and crafts specialist, the Hanukkah assembly, or morning t'fillah (worship).

d. Students, especially younger ones, often spend many minutes each class session waiting to get in line or waiting in line.

e. The last five minutes of the day can be most useful. Use these minutes (clean up and hand out papers prior to this last five minutes) to review, evaluate, pull together the day's learning.

Here are some activities to plug into those moments:

1 *There's a small commercial book,* available in most bookstores, called *The Kid's Book of Questions* by Gregory Stock. (Question #148: If you knew that by cheating you could win an important competition for your school and be a hero, would you? Pretend you were sure you wouldn't get caught.) When you have a spare moment, open the book, read a question and ask the class to discuss. Make a check mark next to the questions you've asked so they won't be repeated. You can create your own book by generating a list of questions that have Jewish content: Who's your favorite Jewish hero? If you could go back in history, which period would you choose? Why? Soon students will be asking, "Can we do a kids' question?"

2 *Flash cards* are versatile and perfect for making the best use of spare moments. Flash cards are great for drill and review. Examples of flash cards: Hebrew letters, syllables, words, phrases. Hold up a card; the student who responds correctly gets to "keep" the card. You can also play "Around the World," which seems to always be a favorite. Practice Hebrew vocabulary. Have flash cards with pictures and ask students to name the picture (in Hebrew).

3 *Singing is a great activity for waiting time,* especially for waiting in a line. Also, some songs and activities are well suited to stretching and providing some active moments for students: Shimon Omer, "Head, Shoulders, Knees and Toes" (in Hebrew).

4 *Twenty Questions*—animal, vegetable, mineral. Topics from the Torah, Ten Commandments, the golden calf, Moses' staff, or harder ones (the sand on the angels' feet). A variation is to designate a specific number of questions students are allowed to ask.

5 *Categories.* When first introducing this game it is helpful to name the category: Sukkot. Students raise their hands to contribute Sukkot words. After a while the teacher can just call out a few words (e.g., ram, idols, tent, guests, angels). Students have to guess what attribute or theme all the words, names, or concepts have in common.

6 *Pictures in a bag.* This can be adapted to many subjects. Example: If you're studying brakhot, fill a bag with pictures of food. Ask a student to reach in, pull out a picture and ask the class which brakhah is the appropriate one to say for this type of food and why.

7 *A "think pad"* is just some small pieces of paper stapled together (good for recycling, using the backs of something else) to make a thin tablet. Kids keep think pads handy. Great for asking students to quickly list something or write three questions about.

8 *Fill a fishbowl* full of quick activities, problems and ideas. When you have a few moments, ask a student to draw a paper from the bowl. The class will then spend the next three to five minutes completing that particular activity. Include: kids' question, flash card games, songs, Bingo, Trivial Pursuit or Jeopardy questions, pictures in a bag, Twenty Questions, Categories.

* **"Ticket out the door"** is a good activity for reviewing, processing, summarizing, or checking for understanding. Students write on a 3"x5" card or just a scrap of paper and hand the "ticket" to the teacher as they leave the classroom. Examples: Write one way you want to be like Noah; list three words to describe an etrog; write four words that describe Abraham; list five ways a family can do tzedakah.

Add it up. Five minutes before class. Five minutes at the end of the day. Five minutes to wait in line, wait for a drink, wait for the art specialist. Fifteen minutes each class session. Multiply by the number of class sessions in a year and then by the number of years a child is likely to be in school. It's a lot of time. Plan for it.

Five Kinds of Seatwork That Make a Difference

I hate seatwork. Kids—and some teachers—call it busy work. It's my belief that kids can zip through what we commonly call seatwork (fill in the blanks, or copy or circle) correctly, yet not really understand key concepts or understand what they're doing. Here are five kinds of "seatwork" that require real work, not just drills. They encourage independent thinking, include higher-level thinking skills, invite students to create their own examples and—an added bonus—can be used over and over just by changing the content.

1 *Writing plays.* Kids use Torah concepts and stories or news articles for content. For inspiration students can look at what Stan Beiner has done in *Sedra Scenes* and *Bible Scenes.* Plays can grow out of studying life-cycle events and holidays. Students create the characters, write the dialogue, develop the scenery and costumes (or puppets), practice the play and stage it for the class, parents or kids across the hall.

2 *Book projects.* Create a class environment that is rich in Jewish books. Get them from your school, synagogue or public library. Have kids bring them from home. Subscribe to a Jewish kids book club. Then create a list of book projects. Projects might include book reviews (based on a one-page format), shoebox dioramas, or story mobiles. Students develop a set of questions for a book and put the questions in a book pocket for future readers to answer.

3 *Lists.* Lists are fun, are quick (sometimes) and can be very creative. In *Managing the Jewish Classroom,* Seymour Rossel suggests asking students to make a "shopping list" for the priests building the Tabernacle, or a "Things-to-do-today" list for a Jew about to be expelled from Christian Spain in 1492. *The Teacher's Book of Lists* offers hundreds of ideas that can be infused with Jewish content.

4 *Games.* Students can develop questions for Jewish Jeopardy, Jewish Trivial Pursuit or any number of other commercial and TV games. These games need dozens (and sometimes hundreds) of questions that children can continually add to until there are enough to actually play the game.

5 *Project cards.* Develop a set of project cards. Use the cases in C. <u>Ha</u> by gluing one case on a card. Students work in pairs or small groups to discuss, research the case, and then check in a separate place for case answers. *Thinker Task Cards* is a Good Apple Creative Thinking Activity Book (found in most bookstores that have an education section) that has two hundred ideas for activity cards that can easily be adapted with Jewish content from your curriculum. Laminate the cards for long-term use.

These types of projects energize kids and move away from boring, drill-oriented seat-work and "sponge" (they soak up the time) activities. Work with a couple of colleagues to develop a storehouse of meaningful, high-level, creative projects that kids can turn to whenever they have time.

Eight Ways to Help Students Retain What They're Learning

Dorothy began teaching second grade just three weeks ago. She's looking for strategies that will help students remember what they're learning—especially in Hebrew classes where she's teaching a letter a week. The kids don't retain what she's taught from one week to the next.

Remembering is a teachable skill. Our problem is that we may only see our students once or twice a week, which makes daily reinforcement and practice impossible.

We know that kids seem to have no trouble remembering football scores, baseball stats, long, complicated raps. Kids unconsciously figure out ways to remember those things that are important to them. We all know that it's easier to retain material that's meaningful.

So, that's the challenge. How do we plan for meaningful learning and find time to practice? What are the conditions that contribute to retention? And what special considerations must we make if we see our students less than three times a week?

1 *Begin with the lesson plan.* Create a performance objective that describes an outcome. Examples:

[a] Students will be able to explain and demonstrate two mitzvot of Sukkot.

[b] Students will be able to properly light a hanukkiyah. It's usually helpful to tell the kids what the objective is—they need to know how their learning fits into a big picture.

2 *Create a set induction* that opens the lesson in a way that both motivates the kids and relates what they will be learning to something they already know or have experienced. When possible, establish links across subjects and with previously studied material.

3 *Model the learning—demonstrate.* Kids learn by watching, observing others, imitating. Have some students model or demonstrate for others.

4 Use of variety of strategies—keeping in mind that kids, like us, have different learning styles. When planning your lessons, design activities that include combinations of tactile, physical, aural, visual, verbal, and nonverbal. Try music, using technology (computers, camcorders, filmmaking) dance, drawing, field trips, dramatization, role play, demonstrations, diagrams, pictures. Bible stories provide excellent opportunities for making learning meaningful. Dramatize the sibling relationships in stories of Cain and Abel, Isaac and Ishmael, Jacob and Esau, Joseph and his brothers.

5 *Use strategies for organizing information in interesting ways:* grouping, categorizing, graphing, time-lines, charts, diagrams, scale models.

6 *Active participation.* Have kids work in pairs or groups to discuss, review, ask each other questions. Those that do the asking tend to be the ones who remember. Putting kids into groups of two or three insures that everyone will participate actively.

7 *Help kids get a visual image.* Hebrew's difficult. So many of our kids bring no background to the learning. To many of our students, the letters may *be Ox House, Camel, Door,* and the *Alef Parent Education Folders* give little stories about the letters that provide wonderful visual images ("Alef used to be an _____"). Kids can act out the letters, create letters from clay or Playdough. (I once saw a classroom set of alef-bet pillows that a parent had sewn.)

8 *Create effective strategies for practicing.* Practice helps kids remember. With our time crunch we need to look for short practice periods:

[a] a quick review at the beginning of the day

[b] quick drills or games between subjects or while waiting in line

[c] meaningful closure at the end of the day

Sometimes there are four or six days between classes. In order to promote retention it's necessary to plan for practice at home. To practice their pronunciation, Jane Golub creates an audio tape that she sends home with all her students. Here's where parents as partners in learning is important. Parents can help provide practice and extension with games and reviews provided by the teacher.

Dorothy has figured it out. Last week she taught the letter *bet.* Students made a *bayit* out of a giant *bet* cutout. They traveled through three learning stations where they: [a] practiced writing *bet* [b] sang the alef-bet song and an old <u>halutzim</u> song about *bet* that Dorothy learned when she was growing up, and [c] played a Hebrew matching game. Students also made a *bet* by pasting macaroni over a large hand-drawn bet and concluded the day with *alef-bet* bingo. The next week parents were invited to do some learning, too.

Five Ways to Help You Think about Your Own Teaching

Every now and then I meet a teacher who knows everything—a teacher who has all the answers. I worry about those teachers. I worry that they are not continually growing, continually looking for ways to become more effective teachers.

Last week I went to a meeting where we talked a lot about reflective practice—thinking about the way we teach and learning how to think about our teaching. We were given several articles about this concept of reflective practice.

A piece by Stephen D. Brookfield (*Becoming a Critically Reflective Teacher*) talks about exploring our teaching by looking at what we do through four critically reflective lenses. They are:

[a] our autobiographies as teachers and learners

[b] our students' eyes

[c] our colleagues' experiences

[d] theoretical literature

While each of these aspects could be the basis of an entire course, I would like to suggest five things you can easily do to help you begin thinking about reflective teaching:

1 *Set aside ten or fifteen quiet minutes at the end of each teaching day.* Use this time to ask yourself questions about that day's teaching experiences. You might have a list of questions that you refer to.

2 *Keep a journal* in which you write down your critiques, questions, notes about particular students, ideas for teaching future lessons, problems that trouble and challenge, strategies that work. Over a period of time you will notice if there are recurring themes and problems that you may want to share with a principal or colleague. You may also want to begin collecting educational articles of interest, notes from workshops you attend, songs, stories, relevant newspaper articles, etc.

3 *Work out a peer/mentoring relationship with a colleague.* Invite your "partner" to observe your class. Talk with her about your teaching plans before class begins. After class, have a conversation about what she saw. Your colleague may see things that you are unable to see and point out things that you didn't know about yourself as a teacher. A colleague/mentor once pointed out to me that I tended to always look toward the left side of the class—a behavior of which I was totally unaware.

4 *Choose some strategies you want to work on and write each on a 3"x5" card.* One week you might want to take special note of children who talk the most. Keep a list. Look at who they are and try to determine if the talking is appropriate, why they talk, when they talk, and develop ways in which they can be redirected, if that is appropriate. Another week you may want to focus on students who talk the least and then devise some strategies for getting them more involved. Another time note the students that you call on. Later note who those students are: All boys? Students who sit on the left side of the room? Those that waved their hands in your face?

5 *Talk with your principal about opportunities for reflective learning and teaching.* Develop a bibliography of articles. Devote a part of every faculty meeting to this notion of *thinking about teaching* as a way of becoming a more effective and continually growing teacher.

Two Sets of Five Ways to Know if You've Had a Successful Day

How do you know you've had a successful day? Sharon Morton asked that question last summer. When I was teaching public school I thought a day was successful if no one cried (including me) or if I didn't have to admit defeat and send a child to the office.

I learned to recognize and be grateful for successful moments. I learned that if we Jewish teachers are truly successful, we may never see the long-term results of that success. Success can include the student who is inspired to continue Jewish learning after high school, the student who has a meaningful Jewish camp experience, the student who becomes a *madrikh*, the *madrikh* who decides to go into Jewish education as a career, and the college student who becomes a lay leader in Jewish education. Those are successes for which we may have planted a seed but which we may never see bloom.

What does success look like in a Jewish classroom? Members of the "Five Things Advisory Group" suggested that you know you've had a successful day if:

1 *It's time to go home and your students don't want to stop working.*

2 *They stay inside from recess to do their work.*

3 *They hug you on the way out.*

4 *They ask, "Can we do this again next time?"*

5 *They come in next time and ask more about the topic you discussed in a previous session.*

Rabbi Kerry Olitzky and Adina Hamik discussed this concept and took it to a more spiritual level.

You know you've had a successful day when:

1 *You can see the sun smiling on the face of a student.*

2 *You recognize that the divine spark in a child has been ignited and his/her soul is set on fire.*

3. *A child offers a Torah insight that blows you away.*

4. *You realize that this is the work you have been called to do.*

5. *You can hear Sinai echoing in your ear in the midst of a daily lesson in class.*

I don't know how you measure that kind of success or if we would even want to. But isn't this why we teach?

Thirty-eight Things About Classroom Management

Five Ways to Get Kids to Line Up

When I began my student teaching experience I was told that the school principal was first cousin to the guy in the school district's hiring office. If the principal liked you, he just called his cousin and—presto—you had a job. Word was that he "liked you" if your students were quiet in the halls.

I quickly became an expert in bribing my first graders to walk quietly in the halls.* That was easy. The tricky part was the part that happens in the classroom—getting those kids in a line before they walk out into the hall. Lines are places where kids are in hitting, pushing and shoving proximity. Lines are places where kids can argue endlessly about who gets to be leader, who "cut," who has to be last. What I learned is that getting into a line provides opportunities for review, grouping, math, Hebrew, singing.

1 *Call kids into the line by groups or subsets.* Line up if you were born in the Hebrew month *Elul*. That group will line up, then go on to other months. Line up if you are wearing clothing that is the color *adom* (red), if you have a *kelev* (dog) at home.

2 *Be the flash card-carrying teacher* (a noncompetitive version of Around the World). Have a set of cards that reinforces whatever you're learning in class. Go around the room, child by child, asking each one to identify the Hebrew letter, syllable, word, phrase. Or have a set of pictures and ask the children to give the Hebrew word. You can use holiday or ritual symbols or a stack of food pictures for which kids must name the appropriate brakhah (blessing). This activity must not punish kids or prevent those who can't answer from going to recess. A rule: The entire class gives the answer when anyone needs help.

3 *Line up if you can tell us:* the name of a city in Israel, a character from the Bible, a letter on the dreidle, one of the four species, your Hebrew name, what you would wish if you had one wish, a blessing that happened in your family, one way to give tzedakah, a Pesah food.

4 *Line up if you have a "bet" in your Hebrew name,* visited Israel, been to a bar mitzvah, two people in your family, two teeth missing.

5 *Sometimes it's possible to have no line at all, especially with older kids.* Use any of the above strategies. As each student responds, he/she just walks to the next venue—library, recess, lunchroom, sanctuary.

* You bet that cousin hired me.

Carol's Ten Least Effective Management Techniques

There's a cartoon that depicts a child coming home from school and proudly announcing, "Daddy, guess what? Just one more check and I get to see the principal!"

Sometimes teachers don't know what they actually accomplish. You've probably heard (or said) the following statements. We all have. The following "strategies" came from the student teachers I used to work with or from students in my class for *madrikhim* at the Community High School of Jewish Studies. In each case, what does the teacher want to accomplish, and what do we think is actually being accomplished?

1 *"If you do that one more time, you'll have to stay in for recess."*

2 *"Josh—what did I just say?"*

3 *"I don't have to be doing this, you know. I could be working at McDonald's and making the same money."*

4 *"I've got all day. I'll just wait until you're ready." (This is accompanied by toe-tapping and arms folded across the chest.)*

5 *"We're all going to sit here until someone tells me who put the graffiti on the bathroom walls."*

6 *"Sarah, you already have twenty-seven checks next to your name."*

7 *"O.K. Alan, (arm thrust toward door) outside!!!!!!"*

8 *"Bob, if you don't put that pencil down right now, I'll take it away."*

9 *"They're not paying me to be a baby-sitter, you know."*

10 *(My favorite least favorite) "If you think you're so smart, why don't you just come up here and teach the class?"*

Let's look at what these techniques really do.

Number 1 and number 8 are threats that punish both the teacher and the student. In number 1 the teacher will have to stay in for recess to monitor the student. And it is usually the student who most needs the outside activity and camaraderie who acts out in class and is told to stay in. In number 8 the teacher has interrupted the teaching to threaten Bob. She will need to follow through, and Bob will need to save face with his peers by tapping longer, harder, or finding some other way to irritate the teacher.

In number 2 the teacher knows that Josh isn't paying attention. Calling on him embarrasses him in front of his peers. And he still won't know what he missed.

Number 3 and number 9 demean the teacher and the teaching profession. Students want to know that their teachers are committed to teaching and love what they do. (About the babysitting comment: There is a Talmudic text that says Torah is too important to become a tool by which people earn a living, thus making it wrong to charge money for Torah teaching. In looking for a way to compensate teachers the rabbis chose to look at Torah teaching as high-quality babysitting. This concept would make a great discussion with older students.)

Number 4 is another surefire looser. Tell students you've got all day and they'll give you all day. They'll show you. What a great time-waster! Maybe they won't have to do any work at all.

Number 5 punishes the whole group for the actions of one (or a few). Kids won't rat on each other. They will sit there all day.

Number 6 is an example of a system that's not working. Even though there may be clearly delineated consequences based on the number of checks a student accumulates, the system may backfire. The system should make it impossible for Sarah to get twenty-seven checks next to her name. In order to save face with her peers, Sarah is going to work on twenty-eight and twenty-nine.

Number 7 accomplishes several things. The teacher admits that she can't handle Alan. Alan gets to leave; that may be just what he wanted. He'll miss out on the learning and will probably find some interesting things to do in the hall. Other students, in order to save face, may refuse to leave the class, stiffen up as you drag them out, or announce loudly that they're glad to leave because class is boring.

Number 10 is another big mistake that takes up class time, gives the class comedian an "open mike," and, in rare cases, may produce a lesson that is better than the one the teacher had planned.

When it comes to class management there are no hard-and-fast rules. It's probably better to follow a small number of basic principles than to always follow a system. The key is to never get to the place where we are threatening our students and engaging in power struggles. We need to build relationships with our students. This is where we will begin next week.

Twelve of Jim Fay's Twenty-three Quick and Easy Classroom Interventions

While I'm driving I listen to a lot of educational consultants and motivational speakers on tape. I get angry with a lot of them. But Jim Fay is different. He is an educational consultant and teacher whose philosophy about children and teaching is very much in sync with mine. His strategies about classroom management center on building relationships with kids. He is concerned about their dignity, their individuality, and their peer relationships. When these concerns color how we deal with kids, we are less likely to get into the threat and power-struggle cycles. Fay believes that it's better to apply a small number of basic principles than to always follow a system. Teachers must not embarrass kids and, at the same time, must not set themselves up for a bad situation. Fay's "Quick and Easy Classroom Interventions" discusses twenty-three classroom disciplinary interventions that move from simple to stronger ones—from the least to the most restrictive. Number 1 is the "give the evil eye" technique. "Send the kid to the principal" is number 14.

For those of you who prefer to read, these same twenty-three steps are included in his book, *Teaching with Love and Logic*.

In between numbers one and fourteen are:

2 *Walk toward the student.* Continue to teach. Don't make eye contact with him.

3 *Stand close to the student.* Continue to teach. No direct confrontation.

4 *Make eye contact.* Gesture "no" with a shake of the head.

5 *A gentle hand on the shoulder of the student.* (Notice that for the first five the teacher hasn't said a word.)

6 *A statement that indicates that the kid is O.K. but the behavior isn't.*

7 *Change the student's location*—the emotional tone is changed at the same time.

8 *Make a statement that indicates the behavior is misplaced.*

9 *Use an I-message.*

10 *Enforceable Statements.* Set limits by describing what you will allow and expect, such as "I listen to people who raise their hands."

11 *Provide choices.*

12 *Remove the student from the group to a time-out.* Student is allowed to return when he can live with the limitations of the teacher or group.

13 *Require the student to fill in a form during the time-out.*

Fay tells wonderful stories and gives many examples for each of the strategies listed above—and the nine that come after "send the kid to the principal." These interventions teach teachers how to engage with children when there's a problem, not move away from them.

Buy the tapes or the book. They'll change the way you think about teaching. The tape comes from *The Love and Logic Press,* 1-800-338-4065; the book you can access through Torah Aura Productions.

Five Reflections on the Privilege of Working with a Madrikh or Madrikhah

This semester I'm teaching at our Hebrew high school. My class is comprised of ten students—grades 9–11— who are *madrikhim*, *ozerim*, or teacher aides in synagogue schools throughout the community. The kids are wonderful. The setup is not ideal because this class is not part of a school's *madrikhim* program, the classroom teachers are not involved, and there is no coordination with the schools where my students are *madrikhim*. Still, I hope that what they have learned from me (and from each other) includes what it means to be a *dugma*, what *madrikhim* do, *madrikhim*-appropriate management techniques, questioning skills, how children learn, and how to plan a lesson.

Mostly, I learn a lot from them. What I have learned is that most schools don't get it. They don't understand the incredible opportunities/benefits that a well-conceived *madrikhim* program can offer.

Here are five suggestions for teachers who have *madrikhim*.

1 *Become a mentor to your madrikh in and out of the classroom.* Coach, teach and facilitate in the classroom. Take a real interest in their lives outside of the classroom. Ask them about their school, their youth group, and their family. Offer to write a college, camp, or Israel scholarship recommendation. Invite your *madrikh* to Shabbat dinner, to help build your sukkah, or to join your family's Hanukkah party. Don't underestimate the impact or influence you may have on the life of a teenage kid or the adult life and career that she chooses.

2 *Your madrikhah may be inspired to become a Jewish teacher.* You are the inspiration. Be the model of an excellent teacher—and let her in on the "secrets." Do your planning and reflection with your *madrikhah*. Look for and create opportunities for her to learn and to teach. CAJE has a teen program and a college program. Invite your *madrikhah* to join you at next summer's conference. Shepherd her through the application process. Your community probably has a variety of learning opportunities for teachers—mini-CAJE, BJE-sponsored workshops, etc. Invite your *madrikhah*—take her to dinner first.

3 *If your madrikh doesn't become a Jewish teacher,* he may very well become a Jewish parent and/or Jewish education lay leader. A positive, inspirational experience as a *madrikh* in your classroom will color the way he parents, lead him in the direction of school board chair when his children are school age, and influence the way he thinks about supplementary schools when he chairs the Federation's allocation process.

4 *Your madrikhah will most likely go to college.* Talk with her about her plans, about Jewish communities and Jewish life at college, about local Jewish organizations (e.g. NCJW) that may offer scholarships to Jewish students. About teaching or tutoring in a Jewish school near the college (after all, she'll have experience and a letter of recommendation from you). Keep in touch with these kids. Help them find the job.

5 *Madrikhim are special—they choose to get up on Sunday morning* (or Tuesday afternoons) and work in your classroom. And I doubt that they do it for the money. They are self-selected—not slackers. While they certainly can help pass out the juice and crackers and supervise recess, they are capable of so much more. Teach them how to tutor in one-on-one situations. Teach them how to lead a small group discussion or game. Teach them how to facilitate a learning center. Teach them how to read a story (with appropriate set-induction and follow-up questions) and give them opportunities to do so.

A *madrikh* experience can influence a life.

When I was a junior in the high school at Temple De Hirsch (before the "Sinai" was added) my principal, Alan Lichter, invited me to become a teacher's aide. I was assigned to a first-grade classroom. Mrs. Berkman was pregnant and, in the middle of the winter, went on maternity leave for six weeks. I got to be the teacher (the sub was my "*madrikh*"). Those six sessions in front of the class influenced my decision to become a teacher.

So it is thirty-five years later. I am still a Jewish teacher. One of my former students funded the first three years of our Florence Melton Adult Mini-School program. One of my students is on my board. Mrs. Berkman's "infant" son is my accountant. One of my students (who claims I always put her in the corner) is the chair of the board of The Jewish Education Council, where I serve as the director.

Five Ways to Use Madrikhim in Your Classroom

Morah Sarah has four <u>H</u>anukkah learning stations in her third-grade classroom. Every student is programmed to rotate through all four centers over the next two weeks. Morah Sarah will work with students at the text station, where they will read about and discuss the <u>h</u>anukkiyah argument between *beit Hillel* (the school of Hillel) and *beit Shammai* (the school of Shammai). She has "walked" her *madrikhim* through the stations. Josh will work with students at the "blessings" station. Shira and her group will play a game based on the Instant Lesson "The True Story of <u>H</u>anukkah." All of them will keep an eye on the fourth station, where students will work independently on an art project.

Last week we talked about the incredible opportunities that a well-conceived *madrikhim* program can offer, emphasizing the role of the teacher in guiding, supporting and mentoring. I talked about the impact of a well-crafted *madrikhim* program on the life (present and future) of the *madrikh* or *madrikhah*.

Today let's talk about the role of the *madrikh* in the classroom. This role looks different in every school. For our purposes we're talking about a model of the *madrikh* in a support role—not an assistant teacher, not a student teacher, and not a person whose sole responsibility is to mix paints, pass out graham crackers, and stand guard at recess. We're talking about a *madrikh* who is part of a teaching team, who is another pair of eyes and hands and ears to observe and listen and provide feedback for the teacher. Using *madrikhim* in the following ways offers you the opportunity to restructure/rethink the way you teach. With *madrikhim* as part of your teaching team your students will be able to participate more actively. They'll have more time on task and more individual attention.

1 *Teach your madrikhim tutoring skills.* It's hard for one teacher to individually help every child in the class. But with a couple of *madrikhim,* one can tutor Aaron in Hebrew while another works with Emily, whose reading is below grade-level and who needs help with her history assignment.

2 *Madrikhim can work on projects with advanced students.* So often we spend our time trying to manage the class and meet the needs of struggling students that we don't have time for those students who are gifted and in need of new challenges. A *madrikhah* can work with a student on a specially designed project or work with a small group in the library.

3 *Madrikhim in the classroom make it possible for you to create a fully participatory learning environment* in which students are working in a variety of groupings: learning centers, stations based on a theme, small groups completing seatwork, two kids studying a text, four students writing a play.

4 *Madrikhim can make mainstreaming successful.* John, from the *tikvah lataf* special needs class, comes into Dorothy's second grade class for an hour a week. Her *madrikh* has been trained to work with John, making it possible for him to spend more and more time with her class.

5 *Madrikhim can facilitate competitions, special projects and programs.* Anne's class created a quilt depicting holiday symbols. Her *madrikhah* worked with a small group from the class to put the quilt squares together and sew the border. Irv's *madrikh* worked with a group of six who are planting trees in the courtyard.

Sam Joseph and Joel Grishaver wrote the book on this stuff—it's called *The Madrikhim Handbook: A Training Program for Teenagers Working In Jewish Schools.* This book is invaluable. It's the textbook for my *madrikhim* class, and I also use it for some of my teacher training workshops (it has a great chapter on the anatomy of a lesson plan). Every teacher needs to have one.

Forty-six Things Effective Teachers Do

What's in a Question? Six Levels from Bloom.

"Rabbi, I have a *she'eilah* (question)."

Asking questions is a Jewish thing to do. Jews ask questions. Frequently we answer a question with a question. Ask two questions at once and the answer is usually "yes." Jewish conversations center on questions.

Questioning is probably the most universal teaching strategy. Effective teachers ask effective questions. Questions need to be clear, simple, purposeful, arranged in some type of sequence, paced to encourage all students to think, and responded to by clarifying, probing, and expanding.

Benjamin Bloom created a hierarchical system that describes six levels of thinking. What follows are Noah questions organized according to Bloom's taxonomy.

1 *Knowledge* (eliciting factual answers, testing recall and recognition). Who was Noah? What does his name mean? What is the name of the boat that God told Noah to build?

2 *Comprehension* (organizing previously learned material in order to rephrase, describe, make comparisons). What kind of person do you think Noah was? Why does the Torah say that Noah was righteous in his own generation? What does it mean to "walk in God's way"? Why did Noah choose a dove? Why did God choose a rainbow to be the symbol of a covenant?

3 *Application* (using previously learned information to solve a problem). What are some things you do when you are "walking with God"? Design a symbol that shows a promise between you and your parents, between you and God. What are we supposed to remember when we see a rainbow?

4 *Analysis* (drawing conclusions, inferences, generalizations; discovering causes or reasons). What is the *shoresh* (root) of the word Noah? Who was comfortable? Who was not comfortable? What is the *shoresh* (root) of *Nahamu* (the Shabbat of Consolation)? Who needs comforting on Shabbat *Nahamu*? How is the story of the flood like the story of creation? In what ways is the flood story the opposite of the creation story? What do you suppose Noah and his family did to pass the time for forty days and nights on that ark? Pretend that you were one of the people on the ark. What would you have done? What would you have said to Noah? God's rainbow message to Noah has three parts. Compare the way each part begins and ends.

5 *Synthesis* (making predictions; solving problems; producing original work). Create a set of blueprints for designing a modern-day ark. What does the story of Noah teach us about conservation and ecology? What solutions would you suggest for saving our world today? After reading what Ramban and other commentators said about the rainbow, create your own midrash about why God chose the rainbow.

6 *Evaluation* (judging the merit of an idea, a solution or an aesthetic work). What do you think is the most important thing to remember about the Noah story? Would Noah be considered a righteous man today? List some people you think would be considered righteous today. What criteria would you use?

Five Questioning Do's and Don'ts

Effective teachers ask questions in ways that encourage all students to think and respond.

1 **DON'T ask a "yes or no" question.** They discourage discussion, encourage guessing, and usually evoke an answer from the class in unison (probably the opposite of the one you want).

DO ask open-ended questions. "Why do you think...? Compare...?

2 **DON'T call on a student first, then ask the question.** (Josh, why do you think...?). Josh's anxiety is raised, and everyone else gets to tune out.

DO ask a question by telling students you are giving everyone time to think about the question (five to ten seconds), then you'll call on a few people. During the "wait time" let your eyes move quickly from student to student. This technique encourages all the students to think about the question.

3 **DON'T just call on students whose hands are waving in the air.** They are always the same people.

DO develop techniques that will help you call on students at random. Students are more engaged when they know they are likely to be called on.

4 **DON'T begin a question with "who can...?"** This phrase sends a message to the class that the teacher expects some students can't or won't know.

DO ask questions in ways that let students know we have expectations that everyone can respond.

5 **DON'T begin a question with "tell me" or "who can tell me."** This encourages students to report to the teacher and cuts the rest of the class out of the conversation.

DO ask questions in ways that include the entire class or group.

Five Strategies for Dealing with Students' Answers

Years ago, Romper Room's Miss Frances asked the studio children what color elephants are. One of the children answered "red." Miss Frances replied, "That's right, elephants are gray." It's not enough to ask questions at a variety of levels. It's not enough to ask questions that are clear, well-paced, purposeful and arranged in some type of sequence. Effective teachers are as careful about their responses to students' answers as they are about how to ask the questions and what kinds of questions to ask.

1 *Giving "think time."* We talked about waiting five to ten seconds after asking a question as a way of encouraging 100% participation. Waiting after a question is asked also encourages students to give longer, more thoughtful answers and to ask more questions.

2 *Using group techniques.* Asking students to respond as a group holds everyone accountable and gives the teacher a way to monitor the whole class at once. Examples: choral response, small group consensus, "whisper to the person next to you."

3 *Probing or prompting questions* that follow the initial response encourage students to go beyond the first answer by stimulating them to think through their answers more thoroughly and extend their thinking. Try probing questions based on Blooms' taxonomy. Examples: "Be more specific," "Explain how," or "Compare".

4 *Reinforcing answers* rewards students for their comments and encourages them to participate more frequently. Reinforcement can be verbal or nonverbal. The most effective verbal reinforcement is complimentary and encouraging. Teacher comments such as "Good thinking," "You explained that well," or "Insightful comment" are more effective than "Good job." Nonverbal reinforcement can be positive (smiling, making eye contact) or negative (frowning, ignoring students, looking bored, passive). Nonverbal messages can encourage or inhibit student participation. Also, a misplaced nonverbal message will displace the impact of an effective verbal message.

5 *Handling incorrect answers.* This brings us back to Miss Frances. This is tricky. Saying "No" or "That's wrong" may embarrass a child, reduce future attempts at offering answers, and negatively affect the other kids in the class. On the other hand, affirming an incorrect answer leads a child to believe that anything he says will be accepted. Positive reinforcement and honesty are both important values. I think we need to separate a student's ego from his answer. What to do? Build on any part of an answer that is correct. Prompt, probe, encourage further explanation.

What could Miss Frances have said in response to the "red elephant" answer? "Perhaps you saw a red elephant in a book or puzzle. Real elephants are usually gray."

Five Thoughts about Praising

This started out as a list of fifty ways to say "wow" and quickly turned into several serious, thoughtful discussions about praise. Teacher praise is the most common form of positive feedback. Teacher praise can make a student feel ten feet tall. "Great job," "I like the way Josh is sitting," "We only need a few more marbles for the jar and then we'll have our class party."

Praising kids is far more complicated than having thirty-two stock phrases to toss out on a regular basis. Praise can be manipulative, patronizing, judgmental, hollow, encouraging, reinforcing, motivating, embarrassing, and even meaningless. Hidden in "You did a great job today" can be "Well, wasn't I doing a great job before?" Inside "good girl" can be "was I a bad girl yesterday?" Offhand comments and bursts of enthusiastic praise can communicate a lot of different things: praise as approval, praise as incentive, praise as bribe, and praise as manipulator. Here are five ways to think about praise.

1 *Think about what you are really trying to accomplish.* Alfie Kohn wrote a book called *Punished by Rewards*. His philosophy is "The more we are rewarded, the more we depend on rewards." He talks about praise as a relationship, a "long-term enterprise of helping children grow into good people." His notions about the three C's (content, collaboration, and choice) fit beautifully into Jewish classrooms where we are trying to build a community.

2 *Think about what you are praising.* Harry K. Wong says we must praise the deed and encourage the student (*The First Days of School: How to Be an Effective Teacher*). He suggests that praise is nice, but not tangible or meaningful. For a more effective kind of praise, point to something the student did well. Then encourage the student to do it again. He lists the following as the simplest yet best rewards: a smile, a high five, a pat, punch or handshake, a word of encouragement, a note or "warm fuzzy," a note home or a call home.

3 *Consider the age of the students.* With older kids praise can be embarrassing. Kids that are publicly praised by their teacher may be labeled as "dorks" by their friends. Sometimes praise given in front of others elevates it to a form of competition. Try talking with students one on one (at the end of class or during an independent work time), thanking them for their thoughtful contribution to class discussion. In many cases private praise demonstrates an understanding of each child as an individual.

4 *Make a conscious effort to keep track of those whom you praise.* Are you praising just the attractive, outgoing kids? Make a conscious effort to keep track of who gets praised (and who doesn't). Brophy (*Learning and Teaching*, page 87)

found that the awarding of praise appears to be contingent on the type of student (bright, attentive, and well behaved) as much as on the answer itself. Teacher expectations have a powerful influence on who and what gets rewarded. Brophy suggests that teachers should:

[a] praise genuinely

[b] praise strategically (be sure the praise matches the achievement)

[c] praise accomplishments that students may be unaware of

[d] praise the effort as well as the answer

[e] praise specifically (praise that depends on and specifies the praiseworthy behavior provides more information than a general response such as "very good").

5 *Realize that the best kind of motivation comes from the student herself.* If teachers can create an engaging curriculum with appropriate activities for each individual child, students will motivate themselves. When each student is provided with an authentic opportunity to learn something meaningful, no external praise will be necessary as a motivator.

Five Meaningful Ways to Praise

When I supervised student teachers at the University of Washington I got my hands on *"65 Ways to Say 'Good for You.'"* The list includes things we all say to motivate the kids in our classes: "That's really nice;" "Keep it up;" "Terrific;" "I'm so proud of you;" "What neat work." Now we have learned that praising kids is a very complicated issue. Yes, we want our students to feel good about themselves. And we want them to be excited about what they are learning and doing. But we also want our words to be meaningful, to change behavior, to help our students move from the need for extrinsic rewards to internal motivation. We need to give them information that makes them aware of why they are successful through comments that describe and reinforce what students have accomplished.

1 *Madeline Hunter* (Discipline that Develops Self-Discipline) *says that messages that have the highest probability of being powerful reinforcers convey three ideas:* "You're competent, you're worthy, and you've put forth effort." Examples: "You've done a great job of sticking to a hard task and finishing it. You should be proud of yourself." "You are really considerate to give your friends time to think." "You really listened carefully to be able to do that." "The record shows you've turned in your homework every day this week."

2 *Give messages to students that define (and reinforce) specific behaviors.* Tell kids why they are successful. Avoid "You did a great job today." (The child might well wonder why yesterday's effort was less than great.) Try "You must have put a lot of thought into your essay. The description gives so many details." Avoid meaningless exclamations—"Super!" "Terrific!" Try "That's a very perceptive comment. You're really thinking." "I bet you're proud of that picture."

3 *When appropriate use nonverbal comments.* A big smile and a "thumbs-up" will convey a message of enthusiasm and support for a child's comment or behavior.

4 *Use anonymous reinforcers.* So many times, without thinking, we tend to say, "I like the way Becky is sitting." This could embarrass Becky or identify her as the teacher's pet. Try "Almost everyone is ready to go to recess—now everyone is ready" or "Some people have already started—they really know how to get to work."

5 *Use Jewish values to highlight appropriate actions:* "You are showing *derekh eretz;*" "You did a mitzvah when you stayed in for recess to help Josh find his lost book."

Joyce Shane, principal of the Seattle Jewish Primary School, has gathered the following Do's of Praise/Encouragement:

[a] Do choose the right time and place according to the preference of the student.

[b] Do use positive language to encourage positive language models in the students.

[c] Do watch your body language: eye contact, smiles, pats on the shoulder.

[d] Do ignore undesired behavior whenever possible.

[e] Do send home a warm fuzzy to the child's parents.

[f] Do use words that highlight a child's developing skills: "You listened and remembered." "You came up with three possible solutions to the problem."

[g] Do praise the small steps students take toward a desired behavior.

[h] Do use words that highlight the linkage between effort and outcome: "You worked hard to finish—now you have free time."

Five Ways to Handle Student Absences

Most of the books about teaching, planning, and organizing focus on record keeping when it comes to student absences. In Jewish schools we do need to keep records, but an absence is an opportunity—to reach out, to build community, to connect with kids and their families—to continue building relationships.

The key notion is to create ways to communicate with the child and to help that child learn what was missed. Even though she is absent, the child is still responsible for the learning. We need to provide opportunities to make sure the learning happens.

Of course, some things can't be made up and it is unreasonable to expect them to be. Particular art projects and most class discussions can't be reconstructed.

1 *Prepared cards.* Design an attractive 5-1/2"x4-1/4" postcard—you can get four postcards on an 8-1/2 x 11" piece of tagboard or cardstock. Whether they are titled *"Refuah Shlemah"* (get well quickly) or some variation of "We Missed You," begin with a pre-printed sentence, then leave room for a personal note from you or from a classmate. Keep a pile of these cards handy and send them out every time a child is absent. If more than two class sessions are missed, take a moment to make a personal phone call to the student and to the parents.

2 *Be sure you know which students have siblings in school* (and which classes they're in). Send homework, "We Missed You" cards, and worksheets home with the siblings.

3 *Keep a Post-it note in your record book that indicates Josh was absent on October 19th* so you will know which papers he didn't do and which discussion or concepts he missed. Take a few minutes when students are working to catch up those who were absent or give needed information to move forward.

4 *Assign study buddies in Grade Three and up.* Each student has a buddy to touch base with in case of absence. Each of the buddies has a responsibility. It is the responsibility of the buddy who is in school to take notes for the buddy who is absent. And it is the responsibility of the buddy who is absent to call his buddy to find out what was missed.

6 *Have carbon paper readily available in your classroom.* This can be used in two ways:

[a] For each class session a person can be assigned to take notes with a carbon and paper underneath. The carbon copy is three-hole punched and placed in a binder, making notes from every session available to all class members.

[b] Send the carbon copied notes home to the child who was absent.

If a child is very ill, hospitalized, or absent over a long period of time, teach the practice *bikur holim* (visiting the sick). Make cards; take small groups (with permission of the parents) for hospital and home visits. Ask for e-mail buddies. Take every opportunity to make the sick child feel part of the class and keep up with the work (if possible). As a class bake *hallah* to take over on Friday afternoon. Take turns calling the student. Make games and puzzles and other activity-oriented gifts.

A FINAL NOTE: Sometimes our kids are absent because they don't take religious school seriously. Our job is to make sure our classes are so compelling that kids won't want to be absent.

Five Things to Include in Your Sub Folder when the Teacher is Absent

I have memories of sneaking into my classroom at 7 a.m., coat thrown over my nightgown, praying that no one would see me. Sniffling, feverish, I quickly threw together some instructions for the substitute and then sneaked out of the building.

When we know we'll miss school there's time to prepare something for a substitute. Whether it's a planned absence or a sudden emergency, being pro-active with a substitute folder that is ready at all times will ensure the best outcome for your class and relieve the pressure of having to throw something together at the last minute. In Jewish schools the sub is likely to be a colleague, the principal, a parent or someone else you know. Your "sub" will be impressed by and grateful for your organization.

1 *Information about the class.* Include a class roster with notes that indicate those students who can be counted on to be helpful; identify any students who have special needs (medical, dietary issues). Include a page that outlines your daily class routine.

2 *Some way of helping the substitute learn students' names.* Keep a set of name tags, table placards or a seating chart in your folder.

3 *Information about the school: emergency procedures.* This should include what to do in case of fire or a seriously ill child. How is recess handled? Snacks? Who are the teachers in the adjoining classrooms? How should serious behavior problems be handled?

4 *Provide two complete lessons.* These should be lessons that have meaning and plan for real learning to take place—but lessons that are not part of your regular curriculum. These lessons will be available in case you have an unplanned absence. Two multifaceted lesson ideas that a sub can just pick up and run with:

> [a] Marc Gellman has a new book called *Always Wear Clean Underwear and Other Ways Parents Say I Love You*. Leave the book (or several of the stories from it) in your sub folder. Design activities that involve reading some of the stories, discussing personal experiences; and adding more ways "parents say I love you". Create a book of ways children say I love you. Write and illustrate a class book called "Ways *kitah gimmel* parents say I love you"; identify the Jewish value on which each story is centered. Write a class letter to Rabbi Gellman with the new suggestions.

> [b] *Bal tashḥit*: waste not. The Jewish concept with roots in Deuteronomy can serve as a springboard for wonderful discussions and projects about ecology, recycling, etc. Check out *Tzedakah, Gemilut Chasadim, and Ahavah: A Manual for*

World Repair by Joel Grishaver and Beth Huppin. Pages 77–80 outline many great projects and concepts on which to base discussions, research, letter-writing, art projects.

5. *Include everything necessary for a class game.* Two ideas:

[a] The Name Game. Write brief bios of famous Jewish personalities (Esau, Henrietta Szold, Rabin) with clues to their identity, listed from general to more specific. Directions to the sub: Divide the class into teams of five or six. Slowly describe one of the famous Jews. The team must work together to figure out the name and then spell it.

[b] The Jewish Star Game. Include in your folder some construction paper and a pattern for making a *magen David*. Students cut out the star and are instructed to write one piece of information in each of the six points (favorite Jewish food, person in history, Jewish book, gift, holiday ritual, etc.), then share the information with each other.

A note to principals: In the school office keep a lesson for each parashah. In case of emergency, substitutes can pick up the week's parashah lesson.

Five Strategies to Increase Active Participation in the Learning Process

It's always the same few students who raise their hands. Many students will tune out of a discussion. These techniques will increase participation (and decrease management problems).

1 *Phrase questions in ways that encourage everyone to do the thinking.* "Think about some of the ways we hurt people with our words. Raise your hand when you're ready with an answer."

2 *Give some "wait time" or "think time" after asking a question.* "Think about some of the ways Jews give tzedakah and then I'll call on a few of you to share your ideas." (Be sure to actually wait a few seconds after asking the question. Scan the room during the "think time.")

3 *Keep a set of cards on which you have written each student's name.* Tell the kids that, in order to make sure everyone gets a turn, they won't need to raise their hands. Ask the question; pull a card from the deck. This one raises the anxiety level a bit. And, of course, if you don't put Bobby's card back in the pile, he's off the hook for the rest of the discussion. But the technique has its place.

4 *Ask kids to "whisper to their neighbor."* (Kids will need to be taught how to do this and to practice the technique.) "Turn to your neighbor and tell each other one of the laws that were taught to B'nai Yisrael. Then I'll call on a few of you to tell us what your neighbor shared."

5 *Have every student keep a "think pad" in his/her desk.* Occasionally you can say, "get out your 'think pads' and list three ways you can show respect for your parents," etc.

Five Strategies for Giving Effective Directions

Teacher to students: "We're going to divide into four groups. Each group will be given one of the Purim mitzvot to discuss and write about. One person in each group will keep a list of all the ideas you come up with."

Teacher to colleagues (after dismissal): "I had a great idea today, but those kids just can't follow directions."

This teacher may have had a great idea, but she didn't do the kind of planning needed to communicate her concept to the class. How will the students know which group they are in? Where each group will meet? What each group is supposed to accomplish? How much time they will have? Is there a minimum number of ideas the group needs to come up with? How do you create ideas about *mishloah manot* (the Purim mitzvah of food gifts)? What is there to say about a Purim *seudah* (the Purim mitzvah of having a feast)? How will each group report to the class?

Directions that are complicated and confusing will need to be repeated. This is a waste of time, energy, and productivity. When students can't follow directions it's usually not their fault. We need to look to ourselves—what do we need to do differently to help kids understand?

1 *Be sure YOU understand the steps needed to accomplish the task.* If you are not clear about what needs to be done, your students certainly won't be clear. If you're planning a game or activity with complicated directions, try it out on a friend, spouse, colleague or one of your own children before presenting it to your class.

2 *Directions need to be clear and concise.* "If you're in the *seudah* group, list on your paper five fun games and activities that can be played at the table." "People in the megillah group need to list eight key parts of the Story of Esther."

3 *Use models or examples.* Show students how to number and list eight items. Demonstrate how to fold the paper and what the finished product looks like. Show them an example of a *shalah manot* basket. Ask a student or two to model the behavior you're explaining.

4 *Put the directions in writing if there are three or more steps.* (Written directions are especially helpful for homework assignments.) Use a chart, diagram, or drawing. For pre-readers, use icons or pictographs.

5 *Check to make sure students understand the directions.* "What's the first thing you're going to do?" Ask students to repeat the directions. If there are three things to remember, ask each of three students to repeat one. Have the class do one of the problems or activities together.

A few more questions to ask yourself before setting the students to work: Do students know how long they have to complete the task? What they're supposed to put in the completed project or paper? What to do after they complete the task? How to get help if needed?

Tools of the Trade: Seventy-five Things to Keep Up Your Sleeve

Five Ways to Create Bulletin Boards If You Don't Have Any (or If What You Have Is Inadequate)

We're talking about the old-fashioned kind—not those that create computer forums for discussion, but those that take thumb tacks, staples, and construction paper. Bulletin boards should be an integral part of the learning and teaching process. Bulletin boards offer opportunities to decorate the classroom, reinforce learning, and display student work. I visit many schools, so I know that many—if not most—teachers are sharing their classrooms with a day school teacher or the Tuesday afternoon teacher, or the preschool that rents the space in the mornings. Bulletin boards (if they exist) must be shared, too. Following are five ways to create space when it seems like none exists:

1 *Use the windows, ceilings and doors as opportunities to display student work.* Ceilings are great for mobiles, windows for painting and hanging artwork, and doors for display and for "take-home" envelopes, attendance charts and the monthly calendar.

2 *Walls, of course!* Where the wall meets the ceiling provides excellent places and spaces for an alef-bet or time-line. Walls are great spaces for maps, charts, diagrams, art projects, photos, and murals. Using tape to affix things to the walls is often a problem. If masking tape won't work, there is a product called "Hold It" that sticks things to walls without damaging the paint.

3 *Use foam core to create your own bulletin boards.* Foam core, found in most art stores, is light, easy to transport or store in a closet or behind a door and can rest in a chalk tray for easy usage. Use duct tape to hinge three pieces of foam core to create a kiosk, or four pieces for a free-standing structure.

4 *Old-fashioned peg board* still provides lots of creative opportunities. It's found at most hardware stores. Buy three pieces and hinge them together. Now you have a free-standing kiosk that provides space to hang games, tapes (in plastic bags), or envelopes that contain seat-work. They also work very well as learning centers. This, too, can be easily folded (although it's less easy to transport) and kept in a closet or behind a door.

5 *Set up a clothesline in your classroom.* With clothespins you can hang artwork, games, posters, book reports, the aleph-bet (each letter on its own card) or develop games and activities that require students to rearrange the cards or pictures to put them in correct order.

Don't overlook a "bulletin board opportunity." Bulletin boards can and should be an integral part of the teaching and learning process. Most teachers spend too much time "decorating" their classrooms. Once you have found or created the space, let the kids do the decorating.

Five Great Party Ideas

Class parties always sound like more fun than they are. Typically, some students are assigned to bring food (candy, popcorn, cookies), and others are asked to bring music. A half-hour "party" can seem interminable when kids are awkwardly standing around without much to say to each other. Try parties with themes that grow out of, or are integrated with, the curriculum.

Following are five great party ideas:

1 *Following the study of Noah in Being Torah,* Cindi Maggied invited her *kitah bet* class to bring their favorite stuffed animals. "Party" activities included learning and singing the rainbow blessing, eating rainbow foods, and reading Marc Gellman's "Rainbow People." In another class Noah students visited the zoo and had a pet-food drive.

2 *At Sukkot ask students to come dressed as one of the ushpizin* (or their significant other/s). It is a Sukkot tradition to invite the Patriarchs, Matriarchs and other "imaginary" guests to join us in the sukkah. Bring a food that person might have liked to eat. (For example, Ya'akov might bring lentil soup; Avraham might bring bread and butter).

3 *Following the study of Va-Yak-hel* (a Torah portion where the Tabernacle is completed), Susan Fish's second graders invited their parents to a "Parashah and Pastry" party at which parents and students studied art and artists and brought "gifts" to the Mishkan for tzedakah. Families took home Va-Yak-hel stories and questions to use for discussion at their Shabbat tables.

4 *At the conclusion of the study of Bereshit* (Genesis), ask students to come as their favorite characters. Each student makes up a riddle about his or her character, and other students guess who they are.

5 *Susan invites residents of Council House as Purim guests.* Students and guests make *mishloah manot* (gifts of Purim food) together. Rivy Kletenik has dozens of Purim ideas. She does theme-centered *mishloah manot*. At Rivy's home guests make up verses and sing grammens (similar to hey lallys) about all the guests as well as characters from the story of Esther. (Ask someone if they know the traditional tune.) Rivy likes to work with her class to come up with theme-centered costumes. Last year Rivy was Cruella DeVil and all the students came dressed in spots. She also suggests eating a meal, not just backwards, but inside out. For example, for dessert try gefilte fish made in muffin cups with _h'rain_ (horseradish) "frosting."

With creative themes, content, food and interesting guests, class "parties"—rather than taking away from teaching time–can enhance classwork and provide opportunities for students to analyze and synthesize what they are learning.

Five Ways to Use the News in Your Classroom

Newspapers provide a living history and lend themselves to dozens of activities and teaching opportunities. Our Jewish classrooms are the perfect places to help students understand issues and how they apply to American Jews. So much of what is happening can be an organic part of your class curriculum. Don't carve out a separate period for teaching current events. Don't save the news for high school students. Integrate the news into all grade levels and all aspects of your curriculum.

1 *Use the news to teach "real world" skills*—to enhance discussion skills and create simulations, to teach and develop analytical and evaluation skills; to identify themes, trends, patterns; to recognize slanted news, bias (there are seven or eight kinds) and propaganda. Compare how different newspapers handle the same story. Those kids who are into cyberspace can check out news online.

2 *Use the news to teach and discuss Jewish values and ethical dilemmas.* What about the teacher who wrote a "reminder note" in felt pen on her student's face? Doctors who use information gathered by the Nazis to solve some of today's medical problems? The plan, of the French synchronized swim team, to perform a Holocaust water ballet at last summer's Olympic games? Ask students to look in the newspaper every day to find examples of modern mitzvah heroes or situations that are waiting for mitzvah heroes to step in.

3 *Use the news to discuss civic issues that have particular interest to Jews*—issues regarding school vouchers; the welfare reform bill that restricts or limits support for certain categories of legal immigrants; hunger and homelessness; ecology and conservation; church and state.

4 *Use your local Jewish newspaper to teach about your community*—its institutions, local happenings and opportunities. How does your Jewish community raise money? What do they do with the money?

5 *Use the news to keep daily accounts of the peace process;* to compare Israeli and American election processes; to discuss how our tradition influences and informs our political attitudes, feelings, and decisions. Display articles the students bring to class. Dedicate one of your learning centers to news activities. Construct a time-line of the peace process or the history of Jerusalem. Choose an individual (Netanyahu, Arafat, Farrakhan) to follow on a daily basis. Simulate a meeting of the Knesset. Save articles that pertain to your curriculum in a class scrapbook or ever-evolving bulletin board. The news bombards our lives and the lives of our kids. Capitalize on it.

Five Things to Consider
When Planning a Field Trip

I asked Josh, age fifteen, to describe the best field trip he ever took with his day school class. Without hesitation he described a trip to see "The Diary of Anne Frank." Why was it so great? The theatre was out of town, necessitating a ferry ride and overnight stay.

Field trips expand the classroom while both enhancing and enriching the learning. In order to be effective they must be carefully planned, with attention given to every detail. They also must relate to the curriculum and be relevant to the interests and needs of the learners. (This week we focus on planning—next week on the curriculum.)

1 *Before the school year begins,* look through your entire curriculum to determine where, when, and how field trips would most effectively enhance learning and understanding.

2 *Be clear about the goals of the trip.* What is the best way to achieve your goals? It may be easier and more cost-effective to bring in a speaker.

3 *Check out the need for reservations, costs* (How will they be paid? Are funds available for students who can't afford?), school policy regarding permission slips and transportation.

4 *Visit the place you're planning to go.* Learn everything you can about logistics and content. Write out detailed instructions for drivers (parents or bus driver), tips for parents, appropriate phone numbers, protocols for lost children (I once lost a student at the National Zoo.)

5 *Prepare students in advance and plan for appropriate follow-up.* Students must know why they are going and what they are responsible for learning.

Five Field Trip Ideas

We began with the check-off list for planning field trips last week. Now we turn to the actual content of the field trip. As Jewish educators, it is important that the trip have significance and meaning, that it relate to the content and curriculum of the class, and that careful attention be given to making the connections. These suggestions are designed to get your thinking started.

1 *Make Jewish field trips Jewish.* Are you teaching about kashrut? Try a kosher scavenger hunt at a local grocery store. Visit a kosher butcher and invite a *shokhet* (kosher slaughterer) to join you. Are you studying Tu BiShvat, ecology, the environment, conservation, endangered species? Visit a rain forest, fish ladder, salmon hatchery. Develop a list of *pasukim* (biblical verses) about animals and create a Torah scavenger hunt at the zoo. Visit a pumpkin farm just before Sukkot.

2 *Will there be an appropriate exhibit at a local museum* (e.g., "Pictures from a Day in Hell")? Call the museum's education department to find out what they can offer in terms of docents, pre-visit study materials, follow-up projects. Check out movies and local theater. (Be sure to see the performance before you take the kids.)

3 *Are you studying the life cycle?* Visit a Jewish cemetery. Gravestones offer a wealth of fascinating information. Visit the mikvah, the Jewish genealogical society. Take your class to a brit, bat/bat mitzvah, shiva house, wedding.

4 *What about current events?* Visit politicians, both Jewish and non-Jewish, to learn about their views on issues that pertain to Israel or affect the Jewish community.

5 *Are you studying your Jewish community?* Check out the local Jewish historical society to learn about their education programs, tours, and archives. Visit other synagogues, the local Jewish newspaper, communal Jewish institutions, and old Jewish neighborhoods.

When you have returned from the trip, who should write thank-you letters? The teacher? The students? The principal? What kinds of activities should be incorporated after the trip to further enhance the learning experience? Remember, field trips are not diversionary experiences or excuses for not teaching the curriculum!

Five Categories of Guest Speakers for Your Classroom

Inviting a guest speaker or teacher can greatly enrich your curriculum. And often it is a better use of time than taking a field trip.

Some considerations: Plan to integrate the guest into the curriculum at the appropriate time. Invite your guest, then follow up with a letter detailing the subject, how it fits into your curriculum, goals, length, and format (lecture, panel, Q and A) of the presentation. Include directions to your school, parking information, name and number of contact person, name of person that will meet and greet the guest upon arrival at the school. Ask your guest to send a résumé or biography. Prepare your class. Tell them who is coming and why. Help them prepare appropriate questions to ask the guest. Plan to introduce the guest professionally and appropriately. You may want your students to wear name tags so the guest may call them by name. After the visit send a thank-you letter and have the class prepare an appropriate thank you as well.

I once hosted a dinner for school principals from Washington, Oregon, Alaska and Western Canada. They were trapped in my kitchen so I asked for help with this column. What follows are thirty guest speaker ideas from twenty-five "experts."

1 *People who have lived history:* Holocaust survivors; participants in Aliyah Bet (illegal immigration into Palestine before there was an Israel); great-grandparents, etc.

2 *People who have Jewish jobs and/or participate in life cycle events:* sofer (Torah scribe), shofar blower, *shohet* (ritual slaughterer), kosher butcher, person who runs a Jewish funeral home, maker of kosher wine, ketubah writer, *mohel* (circumciser), rabbi; a newly married couple; or a recent bar or bat mitzvah.

3 *People who model Jewish values—check the newspaper for stories:* Aaron Feurerstein, who kept his employees on the payroll although the business burned down and they were unable to work; the Giraffes—people who "stick their necks out" for others; Canine Companions.

4 *Jewish artists, craftspeople, musicians:* paper cutters, those who create Jewish ritual items, storytellers, authors, etc.

5 *People who may not be Jewish but offer opportunities to explore Jewish values,* insights, and understandings: zoo people (can talk about what our tradition says about the care of animals), politicians, a person living with AIDS, someone who has a great collection to share (Israeli stamps, coins, rare Jewish books, etc.).

A FINAL NOTE: Dead visitors (what great possibilities). In Anchorage a guy named Gary Zipkin has a Jewish Visitors Program. He writes a script, gets costumes from a local university, contracts with professional make up artists and brings Moses, Golda Meir, and Rashi to class.

Five Things to Do to Use Videos Effectively

Often overheard: "I'm not prepared today—think I'll show a video."

"Great—we don't have to do anything today—she's showing a video."

(I confess. I once showed films for three hours in order to write my report cards.) Videos are a great tool for extending and enriching the learning in your classroom. It's usually best to plan your video schedule at the beginning of the year as part of the overall curriculum planning. Check video catalogues, your synagogue, school, or BJE media center, Blockbuster, et al. Find out how much lead time is needed so you can show your Hanukkah video when you are teaching Hanukkah. This is also the time to plan what content students will need to know in order to be prepared to watch the video.

It's a good idea to plan to be spontaneous. Appoint a parent (or older student) to be the person in charge of home taping for the classroom. Provide her with a bunch of blank tapes. Check the *TV Guide* at the beginning of every week to select shows that you want to have taped for classroom use. Arrange that on occasion you may call to have something taped immediately. With "spontaneous planning" you can bring last night's Larry King interview with Yasser Arafat to class today.

1 *Preview.* Check content. Be sure it teaches what you want it to teach and that it is appropriate for those who will be watching. Make notes that will help you plan your lessons. Note also where it might make sense to cut or skip ahead for the sake of time and where you may want to stop the film for purposes of discussion, to ask students to predict what is going to happen, or to show the next segment at another time. Be very wary of showing commercial-length feature films in class—they are usually longer than the class, with no time for preparation or follow-up—or teaching.

2 *Prepare the lesson(s).* Check to see if there is a commercially prepared lesson. Some feature films come with lesson plans. *"Shalom Sesame"* has a lesson plan for each video in the series. Sometimes lessons are created to help Jewish teachers use commercially made films effectively: CAJE teachers wrote a teaching unit for "The Chosen." Torah Aura has an Instant Lesson to accompany "Schindler's List."

3 *Prepare the machine.* Make sure you have the equipment you need and that you know how to work it. Try it out before the class arrives. Forward the tape to the place you want to begin (classroom management goes out the window if students get to fool around while you're trying to figure out how to work the VCR).

4 *Prepare the class.* Begin with a great set-induction as you would do with any lesson. Students should know what they are going to see and why they are going to see it. You may want to have a set of questions students should keep in mind while they are watching.

5 *Plan for follow-up.* You will want to have several activities, small- or large-group discussions comparing the movie with the book, art and writing projects, and debates.

"Mom, did you know Yasser Arafat was on Larry King last night? Know what he said about the peace process?"

Five Great Classroom Book Projects

Fill your classroom with Jewish books. Create a classroom library. Ask the kids to bring books from home. If your school or synagogue has a library, plan to visit and check out books on a regular basis. When they're in a classroom, most kids associate reading with textbooks. In Jewish classrooms we have an opportunity to demonstrate the joy of reading and learning from Jewish books and to use these books to extend and enrich the class curriculum. Here are five ideas for using Jewish trade books in Jewish classrooms:

1 *Book reviews.* Excitement about books can be contagious. Use student reviews and book projects as ways students recommend books to other students, not just your one-page "book report." Try shoebox dioramas in which students choose a favorite portion of the book to detail in three dimensions within a shoebox. I knew a teacher who used foam core to create a free standing kiosk. She had a pile of 5"x 4¼" cardboard rectangles. Each child used a rectangle to illustrate a favorite book. The rectangles were affixed to the kiosk, which (when folded like an accordion) also served as a room divider.

2 *Mobiles.* Ask students to choose five or six of the most important events from a book to depict on a mobile.

3 *Bookmarks.* Have students choose one key idea from a favorite book and design a bookmark. Use pre-cut sturdy cardboard. Laminate the bookmarks after they are completed. Make a class set of bookmarks. Or have a bookmark contest, choosing several for mass duplication and distribution throughout the school.

4 *Make a book.* Use a familiar story format for the creation of class books, in which each student makes one page. Example: Use *A Sense of Shabbat* as a model for creating new books—*A Sense of Pesah, A Sense of Shavuot*, etc. After reading and discussing *A Sense of Shabbat*, as a class determine what holiday your book should have as a focus. Each child writes and illustrates one page. You can build an entire library of class-made books. A variation of the class made book is the class *milon* (dictionary). Every time a new word is learned, a student writes and illustrates a new page for the class book. This is also neat for creating a class Alef-Bet book. Each page has a huge letter on the bottom. Students write and illustrate words on the appropriate page. At the end of the school year the class books can be donated to the school library. Make sure each is appropriately catalogued so other students can check them out.

5 *Make a Big Book* in which young children illustrate oversize pages and the teacher writes (in very large print) a sentence (using the child's words) under each picture. Or make a class dictionary in which each child writes and illustrates a word, concept, value, or holiday from the curriculum. Sometimes it's fun to have older students make "Big Books" for the kindergarten class.

Five Ways to Use Jewish Books

At our workshop at CAJE, Deena Bloomstone created a "five things" piece on Jewish books. Deena is a Torah Aura author, a member of our "Five Things advisory group," and, as of this writing, is about to become the Education Director of Temple Beth Avodah in Newton, MA. Here are five ideas for using Jewish books in our classrooms. Thanks, Deena!

1 *Book gifts:* Marcia Goren Weser, a Gimmel-level Hebrew teacher, gives books for work well done. Students are excited about receiving their books and they often speak with Marcia about the books once they've read them.

2 *Read in class:* Every class session, devote some time to reading a book to the class. This could take place anytime during the session. I recommend the last fifteen minutes. You can read a chapter a week and have students create a poster listing the books the class has read throughout the year.

3 *Assign reading:* Middle school and high school students often need to read books of their choosing and write reports on them. Promote the reading of books with Jewish content. They will not only receive credit in secular academics, they will have read a Jewish book.

4 *Books on tape:* An ambitious project to do with upper-grade students is books on tape. As part of our mitzvah day activities, our congregation has tape recorded books for the visually impaired. Taping books requires some rehearsal, but I've found students don't mind because they are doing something to help others. A word of caution, though. You might want to contact the publishers of the books you are taping so they know why you are doing it.

5 *Book contests:* Hold your own book-reading contest in school. Provide each student with a list of ten books. Lists should be grade-appropriate. Promote the contest to families. You might consider including the entire family in reading the books. Make a deadline toward the end of the year. The class that completes the reading list or reads the most books receives a certificate of completion and possibly a class party.

Five Great Ways to Teach and Learn with the Jewish Internet

I am awestruck by the Internet. I'm not a maven. And I don't spend hours "surfing the net." But, I am amazed by the breadth and diversity of resources available to Jewish educators through the Internet.

"The Greatest Gathering of Jews Since Sinai." That's how Jewish Web Week was billed in February 1998. It's a Jewish cyberfair, a global online celebration of the Jewish Internet. Jewish Web Week changed my life. I had never spent much time on the net. I don't surf. But in preparation for that year's Jewish Web Week column, I surfed.

I began with the Jewish Web Week site and just clicked as the idea moved me. Clicking onto JewishGen, I read about the annual Jewish genealogy conference, registered online, and never looked back. In Los Angeles for the conference, I called relatives I had never met. Those relatives called or "found" others. Now there is an entire family of Jelikovskys planning a "reunion" this summer. It could happen to you.

During Jewish Web Week 1999 I learned that the Internet is a mecca for Jewish teachers. If you have not used the Internet as a resource, Jewish Web Week is a good time to explore because many of the Jewish sites gear up with special educational events and projects. Starting with The Jewish Web Week site to see what was happening, I found a special online discussion to explore issues related to integrating technology into Jewish education. I could join in the discussion with questions or experiences I have had using technology or just "lurk" and listen to the conversation. The education "channel" on the Jewish Web Week site was sponsored by the Jewish Educators Electronic Toolkit, which is a project of the Jewish Education Service of North America (JESNA).

For several years I've had a Jewish teacher fantasy. I pictured myself, the queen of procrastination, late at night, downloading great lesson plans from the Internet, walking into class the next day, armed and ready to do great teaching. It won't work. Beside the fact that having a great lesson plan doesn't necessarily make for great teaching, you can get lost in Jewish cyberspace. I did.

Below are five favorite categories of Jewish web sites for teachers. Let me know where your surfing takes you. You might find a whole new family.

Jewish Stories

1 *At Bubbe's Back Porch* (http://www.bubbe.com) hang out with Bubbe and tell Jewish family stories. Bubbe sponsors the Digital Story Bee, which is based on the concept of the old-fashioned quilting bee. But here you weave family stories and photographs. Folks in Tel Aviv, New York, San Francisco, Palo Alto, Kiev, Moscow and St. Petersburg gathered for an online workshop during Jewish Web Week 1999.

2. *My Jewish Community—An Internet Lesson* (http://www.bjesf.org/MAIN/BATTAT_CENTER/JEO_CBank/IDENTITY/MJC.FALL.96.html) provides a project for students to learn about their community and publish the stories on the Internet.

3. *Symphony of Candles* (http://www.symphonyofcandles.com) is a gorgeous site. Laura Stein and Jason Turbow took a two-year journey to study Shabbat in diverse communities around the world. This beautifully photographed project is a work in progress. I was moved by Sari's Story. Sari lives in Northern California and knows no greater joy than spending Friday evenings with her children. But Sari knows this joy every other week because her children spend alternating weeks with their father, who is not Jewish. Through photographs and essays, as well as Internet-hosted audio and video, *Symphony of Candles* will present a two-year study of Shabbat and the people who "keep it close to their hearts."

Jewish Fun, Games, and Holidays

1. *Dr. Nurity Reshef's "Jewish Funland"* (http://www.bus.ualberta.ca/yreshef/funland/funland.htm) presents a number of Java-enhanced instructional games including Jewish Funland, Tu-B'shvat, and a Noah Quiz. Also, look for the "One Hundred Years of Zionism" quiz show.

2. *The Bureau of Jewish Education of San Francisco, The Peninsula, Marin, and Sonoma Counties* has a great online curriculum bank (http://www.bjesf.org/MAIN/BATTAT_CENTER/JEO_CBank/CBank.html) where I found a wonderful Tu B'Shvat "How To" (http://www.bjesf.org/MAIN/BATTAT_CENTER/JEO_CBank/HOLIDAY/TuHowTo/TuHowToIndex.html) booklet.

3. *Holidays on the Net* (http://www.holidays.net/), sponsored by *The Jewish Post of New York* Online, is a site that includes information about many different holidays. Their archive on Purim offers a selection of activities, including a "downloadable" grogger that can be used when reading the Purim story. The site also provides instructions on making your own grogger, a hamentaschen recipe and some background on why we dress up in costumes and wear masks on Purim.

4. *The Pedagogic Center of the Joint Authority for Jewish Education in the Diaspora in Israel* (http://www.jajz-ed.org.il) provides educational resources and curriculum on all the holidays and much more. And don't forget *Torah Aura Productions* (http://www.torahaura.com) welcomes guests and introduces new curriculum, stories, and authors. Here's where you can find back issues of the *Torah Aura Bulletin Board* and the "Five Things" columns.

Jewish Indexes

1 *I tried the Alta Vista search engine* (http://www.altavista.com), but any other search engine will do the same. Enter the word Purim (or anything else Jewish). It will take you everywhere.

2 *Here are five books about the Internet:* The Guide to the Jewish Internet by Michael Levin (software is included). *New Kids on the Net: A Network Sampler* (Internet Activities for K-12) by Sheryl Burgstahler. *Judaism on the Web* by Irving Green. The *Jewish Guide to the Internet* (2nd edition) by Diane Romm. *The Prentice Hall Directory of Online Education Resources* by Vicki Smith Bigham and George Bigham.

3 *Click on "Jewish Children's Website Guide"* (http://www.geocities.com/ Heartland/Plains/7613/) for a listing of sites, including Torah Tots (http://www. torahtots.com)—the site to find printable coloring and puzzle pages about prayer and Torah, and detailed, fun Torah synopses for young children.

4 *The Jewish Web Week* (http://www.jww.org) site is a major hub of Jewish activity each February.

5 *The Maven "virtual know-it-all" index* (http://www.maven.co.il) provides a searchable database of everything Jewish from A to Z.

6 *St. John's University* publishes a listing of links to a plethora of Jewish sites (http://www.stjohns.edu/library/staugustine/JewishStudiesTOC.html). If you are searching for almost anything Jewish, you can find a link here. The site contains other search engines, such as Maven: The Ultimate Jewish Search Site. There are listings of Holocaust reference sites, many Torah commentary sites, etc.

7 *The Ultimate Jewish/Israel Link Launcher* (http://ucsu.colorado. edu/~jsu/launcher.html) is a site with more than 4,500 links to a variety of Jewish web sites. A good place to start.

8 *General web sites of interest to Jewish teachers and parents include* Scott Mandel's home page, "Teachers Helping Teachers" (http://www.pacificnet. net/~mandel/index.html), which provides valuable lessons and Internet links. Teach with Movies (http://www.teachwithmovies.org) uses movies as a parenting tool. Created by Jim Frieden and Deborah Elliott, this site include guides for 150 movies, focusing on values.

Talmud Torah and Online Learning

1 *The Jewish Youth Leaders Forum* (http://www.jewishyouth.com/) is a good resource site. Lots of educators sharing ideas. They publish an e-mail list that is interactive; people make queries about programs or topics, others reply.

2 *JUICE, the Jewish University in Cyberspace* (http://www.wzo.org.il/juice/index.htm), offers online undergraduate-level education in Judaica (history, text, etc.) A good place for ongoing education for teachers or supplemental information for their classes. Some of the courses they have taught include Medieval Jewish History: Jews and World Civilization II; An Introduction to Jewish Law; Jewish Underground Movements in Pre-Israel Palestine; The Talmudic Mind; and Family Relations in the Bible.

3 *Zipple.Com* (http://www.zipple.com) opened earlier this year. It's about everything Jewish. Categories include anything from Arts and Humanities to Travel. Being a teacher, I checked out the education section. There are lectures on the weekly Torah reading by the faculty of Bar-Ilan University. Their Purim materials include pieces on "Reciting Hallel on Purim" by Rabbi Judah Zoldan and an article on the "Laws and Customs of Purim" by Naftali Stern. There are four articles on Parashat Tetzaveh.

4 *Navigating the Bible* (http://bible.ort.org) is a project of The World ORT Union. (I was visitor 114,247.) This project has been developed to "allow all people across the globe to be able to read, study and enjoy the Bible." It is clearly a great tool for bar/bat mitzvah study. Each torah portion is chanted by a professional cantor—it's virtual bar mitzvah training.

5 *Torah on the Information Superhighway* (http://www.torah.org/) is a great resource for Torah and commentary, with lots of online classes. Check out the online menorah, which is "lit" each day of Hanukkah.

Jewish Communities

1 *Virtual Jerusalem* (http:// www.virtual.co.il/) is your guide to Jerusalem. As a first-time visitor I had to try out the "Kotel Kam," where you can see what's happening at the Kotel this very moment.

2 *If you teach Israel,* check out (www.israel-info.gov.il). The Israeli government's information site is a great resource for teachers. It's from the Ministry of Foreign Affairs and includes all kinds of facts about Israel, from biblical times to the present; Israeli-Arab relations and the peace process; much information about the government of Israel—its ministries and agencies; policy speeches; interviews and briefings by Israeli leaders; education and student programs in Israel; maps and pictures.

3 *Generation J* (http://www.generationj.com) is a new website sponsored by UJA Federations of North America, it is billed as the magazine for today's Jewish Gen-Xers. The site includes topics on Health and Fitness, Young Parenting, Relationships, Spirituality, Social Action, Lifestyles, Culture and Politics. A Poetry Slam area invites participants to submit their own poetry and offers readers an opportunity to vote. There's also a Café J chat room.

4 *Jewish Family and Life* (http://www.jewishfamily.com), developed by Yossi Abramowitz, offers much for Jewish educators and families—from recipes and basic brakhot to discussions about Jewish values and Jewish health issues.

5 *Reading the Jerusalem Post* (http://www.jerusalempost.com) online is one of the best ways to keep informed about Jewish current events, especially those in Israel.

Flashcards: Five Activities

Every teacher should keep a stack of blank index cards. Use flashcards to review, to reinforce, to summarize, to memorize. Use flashcards between lessons, for independent practice, to close a lesson, to end a day. From Gan through high school, to teach Mishnah, brakhot, holiday symbols, Hebrew. Quiet indoor activities, noisy outdoor relays.

1 *Judy Miller's Gan teachers use Hebrew flashcards to play Tic-Tac-Toe.* After students have learned a few letters, the class is divided in two teams—x's and o's. The teacher holds up a flashcard. If a person from x team correctly identifies the letter, she puts an x on the Tic-Tac-Toe board in the place of her choice. Students learn how to identify letters, take turns, and play Tic-Tac-Toe—all at the same time.

2 *Post a question on the board.* As students come into class each takes a blank flashcard and writes his or her answer to the question. This can be used as a set induction or as an activity for the on-time students to do while the others arrive.

3 *At the end of class, ask students to write a two- or three-sentence "I learned..." statement* and sign the card. (They can also put questions and feedback on the card.) At the beginning of the semester, let students know that you will read the flashcards regularly. At the end of the semester the instructor can use the cards as a tangible way to double-check attendance or as a prompt for report cards that need to include a written narrative.

4 *Write a question on each index card.* Write the answer to each question on the back of a non-matching question card. These cards can be used in several ways. Ask Sandy to read her question. All students try to answer. The person who has the "right answer" then confirms and shows her card. Or Mike asks his question. Everyone looks on the back of his or her cards. The person who has the "right" answer reads it aloud. The rest of the class can agree, disagree or discuss.

5 *Bina Guerrieri uses flashcard activities in her Total Physical Response (TPR) approach to teaching Hebrew.* Spread flashcards on the floor or anywhere in the room. Give commands to different students to point, to sit on, to hop on one leg, hold hands with two friends and run to the word _____. The teacher may call on a particular table to do an action—e.g., "Table #2, please walk slowly to the word _____, pick up the word and read it out loud." "Please put the word *b'shivtekhah* on David's head, back, etc." If the topic is classroom objects, commands will include these objects—e.g., "Go to the chair, pick up the word for God, put it on the siddur and read it."

Some years ago Nancy Messinger wrote *Flashcard Ideas for Teaching Hebrew* in CAJE's Bikkurim. Send a posting to <www.caje.org> for the exact issue. Check your library for "Secrets of a Flash Card Carrying Teacher," from *Instructor Magazine*, October, 1983.

Five Great Classroom Projects

Midwinter—after the excitement of Hanukkah and winter break and just prior to gearing up for Haman and groggers—is a good time to begin a new project. A carefully crafted project can transcend several areas of your curriculum, build community, involve families, weave together two or more areas of study, actualize values you are emphasizing, apply what students are learning in class to real-life situations.

Here are five projects that center on Torah, Jewish identity, history and citizenship, tzedakah.

1 *Susan Fish designed "Noah and the Great Zoo Project"* to focus on her second grade's study of *Bereshit, Noah* and *Lekh Lekha*. The project includes study of the *parashiot* (Torah portions). It integrates several areas of the curriculum, builds community, and creates a new avenue for tzedakah. The class learned how to care for animals, studied mitzvot related to animals and talked about animal research. Integrated into the study was Hebrew vocabulary, stories, songs, games, word study, reading and writing—all centered on animals. After a visit from the King County Humane Society, complete with guests (a very special golden retriever), students elected to use their tzedakah for a class pet-food drive. They also donated two "Caring for Animals" quilts to the Humane Society to thank them for their informative visit.

The culminating family experience (open to siblings and grandparents, too) was designed to celebrate the *parashiot* and involve families in the learning. Families met on a Sunday afternoon at the Woodland Park Zoo. They picked up their "research" packets and maps and began their tour and discoveries of the zoo. After an hour the families met together to read the *parashiot*, midrashim, and stories, followed by snacks, singing and dancing.

2 *Paul Epstein and Moti Krauthammer created a Jewish photojournalism project.* Class discussions centered on what it means to be a Jewish artist and what it means to photograph Jewish subjects. They also discussed and analyzed professional photographs of Jewish subjects. Each student was given a roll of film and assigned to create a Jewish photo essay. Shawna photographed a day in her own life. Josh took a series of photos during his family's seder. One student took photos, titled "Zionism and Terrorism," through a series of chain-link fences. Another photographed all kinds of Jewish lights, while another documented Seattle's massive "Israel at 50" celebration. One of the photos was chosen to become the cover of our Hebrew High catalog.

3 *Shaya's U.S. Government class at the Northwest Yeshiva High School not only learned about local and national government structures,* they had an incredible opportunity to teach what they learned and to learn from a completely different perspective. Shaya's teacher arranged for the ninth graders to tutor a class of Vietnamese adults for their citizenship tests. The students made a series of visits to a local Asian counseling and referral service. The high school students learned that citizenship tests are comprised of one hundred questions (and, of course, had to learn the answers themselves) ranging from the colors on the U.S. flag to questions about the names of the mayor, governor, highest U.S. officials and most important rights. In addition to the tutoring, the high school students spent time talking with their adult "students" and had an opportunity to see what U.S. citizenship means to new immigrants.

4. *Each year for Earth Day Judy Miller's students paint clay pots with bright colors, plant geraniums* in them, and take the pots to the Jewish Retirement Center in Tulsa. Her students talk with the residents, sing songs, exchange stories.

5. *Linda Kirsch's school is in the process of creating an illustrated school Torah.* It's a three-year project for their Sunday Judaica School students in grades pre-K through five. Students measured the height of one of the temple Torahs to use as a model for size. On Sim<u>h</u>at Torah each year, each class gets a summary of "their" assigned Torah portion and a sheet of paper approximately 18" high and 27" wide. The class discusses the Torah portion and brainstorms ideas on how to best illustrate it. Older students may use essays or poems. Younger classes use pictures. Everyone participates, and everyone's name is on the work. Three senior adults made *atzei hayyim* (the wooden rollers) and the mantle and helped put the sections together. Each year's section is laminated. The first two years are now complete. The year 5760 will bring an illustrated Torah that approximates the height and weight of the synagogue's large temple Torah. The illustrated Torah was unrolled this past Sim<u>h</u>at Torah, displaying the first completed section (eighteen *parashiot*). Children found the parts they had created and talked about the stories they told.

Five Great Tzedakah Projects

Maimonides' ladder. Siegel's mitzvah heroes. The little brown envelope.

Every school has tzedakah programs and fairs. Every class has some tzedakah collection ritual. If you're looking for new ideas and projects, here are five that were submitted this week.

1 *In Judy Miller's day school, the math teacher co ordinated a special tzedakah project for the "100th day of school celebration."* They brought in one hundred various items to donate to local shelters. They collected bars of soap, cans of food and toothbrushes. The children grouped items by fives and tens to count things as they were packed, integrating math and Judaic studies. This one has dozens of possibilities across ages and settings.

For example, Idie Benjamin's Girl Scout troop (which is sponsored by their day school) has another idea. For the Eighty-fifth anniversary of Girl Scouts (pick any number) they collected eighty-five children's books for a clinic and eighty-five pieces of winter clothing for a shelter.

2 Last week Elana Stiefel became a bat mitzvah. *For her tzedakah project she collected children's books from family, friends, and neighbors.* The books were arranged in beautifully wrapped baskets that served as centerpieces for the kiddush lunch at the synagogue and then delivered to women's shelters and homes for abused women.

3 Here's a good one for older students. *Require everyone in the class to have a pencil.* If a student forgets, "sell" him/her one for fifty cents that goes to the class tzedakah fund. This is a good way to insure that most of the students are prepared most of the time and to transform a "mistake" into a positive action.

4 Danny Siegel sent a posting this week about about *Asmare Teshome Adem, a ten-year-old Ethiopian boy whose family has not been allowed to submit an aliyah request to the Israeli Embassy.* He and his family are starving. They receive no assistance from the state of Israel or the JDC. Have your students go to the website, <http://www.circus.org/shanda.htm>. Read Amare's story and become part of the letter-writing campaign to help those Jews who are stuck and starving in Ethiopia.

5 *Dorothy Finsel found the "Homelessness Simulation Game" on the Internet.* It's created by Glenn Stein of the Religious Action Center of Reform Judaism. The game is best for high school-age kids (and older) in small (a dozen) or huge (two hundred) groups. The website includes full description and details. Check out <http://www.ajritz.com/jew/homesim1.htm>

One Project: Five Stories

Dorothy Glass does a special tzedakah project. For Hanukkah she gave each of her second-grade students two things: a personal card saying that $1 had been donated in his/her name to the Jewish Federation's campership fund, and a dollar bill attached to a "tzedakah certificate."

The front of the tzedakah certificate: "This dollar is yours to give for tzedakah in any way you choose" with a quote in Hebrew and English from *Pirke Avot* (*al shlosha devarim*): "The world stands on three things, Torah, Worship and Acts of loving kindness" (1.2).

The back of the tzedakah certificate: "A few things to remember. When you give to someone or help someone, you should do it cheerfully and graciously. It is best to help someone without telling lots of people because you might embarrass the person you helped. The greatest act of tzedakah is to help someone help themselves."

Students were instructed to complete the "certificate" by answering these three questions: What did you do with your tzedakah money? How did it make a difference in someone else's life? How did it make a difference in your life?

1 *Sam told his public school class about the project. He convinced his class to adopt a family for the holidays.* Sam put his dollar and $10 of his own money toward the support of this family.

2 *Marisa gave her dollar to a homeless musician who was playing a guitar outside the Pacific Science Center.* This prompted a spirited class discussion about homelessness. Marisa's classmates asked her: How did you know the man was homeless? Why is that tzedakah?

3 *Raymond attached his dollar to the outside of a tzedakah box that he took to the temple's family Hanukkah dinner.* He walked from table to table and collected $22 that he sent to victims of Hurricane Mitch.

4 *Pete told his mother he wanted to use his dollar to buy something at the grocery store to take to the food bank at Jewish Family Service.* Pete learned that there was hardly anything you could buy for a dollar. He ended up spending $15 of his own money.

5 *Yu Xin bought wax with his dollar.* With the wax he made candles. He sold the candles for $5 each and grossed $1,000. With the $1,000 he bought a wheelchair, which he sent to his handicapped friend who lives in an orphanage in China.

The power of discussion. The power of a dollar. The power of creativity and entreprenuership. When we climb Maimonides' ladder, we end up in a place much higher.

Five Ways to Celebrate the Accomplishments of Jewish Women

"If only more of our unwanted children could be placed in the care of loving parents who would give them normal family life, they would grow up to be decent citizens. And we would never see them in court." (Justine Wise Polier, first woman ever appointed as a judge in the State of New York.)

Congress has proclaimed March as Women's History Month. It's appropriate for Jewish educators to use this proclamation as an opportunity to focus on and celebrate the accomplishments of Jewish women. You need not narrow the celebration to March—it can be another month or an all-year study.

Women of Valor is an exciting national project that should serve as a resource for your projects, programs and celebrations. *Women of Valor* is a joint project of The Jewish Women's Archive and Ma'yan, the Jewish Women's Project in New York. Its goal is to highlight the lives and achievements of Jewish women. The collaborative project centers on the production and dissemination of posters and resource guides. Posters are available showcasing Glikl Bas Judah of Hameln, Rose Schneiderman, Henrietta Szold, Molly Picon, Rebecca Gratz, Lillian Wald, Emma Lazarus, Hannah Greenebaum Solomon, and Justine Wise Polier. Each beautifully designed poster features the story of one of these women's lives, using her own words to create a picture of her achievements and the times in which she lived.

The following projects grow out of and are inspired by the work of the *Women of Valor* project.

1 *What qualifies a person to be selected for celebration?* Have your class create a set of guidelines. Based on those guidelines, nominate, discuss, and select a Jewish woman (or several) and design your own posters. To make this an all-school project, each class could select one woman and create a poster. All the posters then become part of a school-wide or synagogue-wide exhibit or Wall of Fame. The project could become a traveling exhibit, moving from class to class on a rotating basis or even to other schools or synagogues in the community (or to your pen-pal school in another state). Or it could become a virtual exhibit on your school or community's website.

2 *Oral history project.* Discuss and select local Jewish women to celebrate. Invite each woman to tell her story to your class. Videotape the visits to show as part of an all-school event or culminating class project and then donate the tape to the library or to the local Jewish historical society.

3 *Select a theme for every month—history, politics, the judiciary, music, art, holidays, etc.* Study and read about one or several Jewish women who have made their mark in this particular area.

4 *Based on a set of class-developed guidelines, choose a famous woman from every century* or from different contexts—historical and modern women of Israel, women of the Bible, women of the Talmud, etc. Create a bulletin board, quilt or poster exhibit.

5 *Choose one famous Jewish woman that the whole class studies.* Each student then is assigned to celebrate the woman in a different way—through art, poetry, narrative, diorama, drama, debate, music, etc. This could become an all-school project in which each class studies and celebrates one woman, bringing all the projects together to form a living museum.

Your celebration of Jewish women need not be relegated to the month of March. You might choose *Kislev* and begin with a study of Judith. Or *Adar* and begin with Esther. Or *Nissan* and begin with Shifrah and Puah, or Yoheved and Miriam. Jewish women can be an ongoing, all-year focus.

"The highest and best that we desire we can only accomplish when men and women work hand-in-hand together. Even Paradise was not complete without a woman, and no paradise on earth can be perfectly complete unless we have men and women" (Hannah Greenebaum Solomon).

Five resources to inform and inspire your projects:

1 *Jewish Women in America: An Historical Encyclopedia*, edited by Paula E. Hyman and Deborah Dash Moore.

2 The Jewish Women's Archive, "the world's first and only archival, research and educational center dedicated to preserving and making known the history of Jewish women." <www.jwa.org>

3 Two curricular pieces that focus on women. *Jewish Women*: A mini course by Sandy Eisenberg Sasso and Sue Levi Elwell, published by A.R.E., 1986. *The Three Pillars: A Book for Jewish Women* by Deborah M. Melamed. Published in 1927 by The Women's League of the United Synagogue of America. Both of these pieces reflect the times in which they were written. Comparing these two curricula with the curricula from the *Women of Valor* project would create a fascinating discussion.

4 *Listen to Her Voice* by Miki Raver, Chronicle Books.

5 *The Invisible Thread: A Portrait of Jewish American Women*, Jewish Publication Society, 1989.

Seventy-five Things for Holiday Celebrations

Five Jewish Calendar Activities

We center our lives in Jewish time. As teachers, we want to do everything we can to lead kids and their families toward lives that revolve around Jewish days, Jewish weeks, Jewish months, Jewish years.

1 *Moonrise.* Dan Bender lives in Hawaii. He submitted some ideas that he and his wife do with first graders. "We go out to the beach at night (most kids live near a beach), and we wait for the moon to rise. We ask the children to observe the moon and make a chart of their observations during a four-week period. Parents are invited to help. Then we pose a question: Do you see a pattern? We explain: This is our Jewish way of using the pattern of the moon to set the times for holidays, and for crops, and for catching fish (fish bite just following a full moon). We ask the children to imagine that they are in the desert (like the Hebrews in Egypt). How would you know what the date is? What questions would you have? How would you tell others about the moon phases? What is another name in Hebrew for moon? First graders are taught patterns in other lessons, so looking for patterns of the moon makes it easier for them to get into the calendar and into the patterns in Jewish life.

2 *Calendar Wheel.* Sue Littauer writes that at Temple Beth El the second grade classes do a calendar wheel. Each child makes a laminated wheel that shows the correspondence of the Jewish months to each season and each holiday in the quarter.

3 *Moonwatch.* Second and third graders love to do a one-month moon watch, marking the progress of the moon's waxing and waning. You can tell which sliver of moon is beginning the month (rather than ending it) because it is shaped like the letter *resh*, as in *"Rosh hodesh"*, or "Right side". Likewise, the sliver of moon at the end of the month is on the left, like the arch of the letter shin, as in *"rosh hodeSH"*.

4 *How big is 5759?* Have kids add beans to a jar each day and count how many they put in as they go. When the jar fills, figure out how many jars it would take to represent the number of years on the Jewish calendar.

5 *Seasonal Effect.* Julie Katz suggests that a fascinating discussion for teens and adults is one that compares the Jewish calendar to the Islamic calendar. The Jewish calendar is luni-solar and has a rather intricate system of leap years/months. The Islamic calendar does not—and the effect of a non-adjusted calendar is that Islamic festivals can fall at any time of the year. It can make a big difference, for example, if you have to fast for Ramadan in July versus in December, with its shorter days. This brings up some interesting questions: What might it be like to have Pesa<u>h</u> in November? <u>H</u>anukkah in June? Sukkot in July? Does season affect meaning? How? If you live in a part of the world whose seasons do not match up with those intended for Jewish holidays (based on Israel's seasons), do you have some holiday traditions based on that climate? Could you create some traditions that might complement those already in place? What is the relationship between nature and religion anyway?

Five More Jewish Calendar Activities

We received dozens of great calendar ideas and projects. Last week we talked about projects related to Jewish time. This week we talk about activities that center on the Jewish calendar.

Every classroom should have a Jewish calendar as an integral part of the room environment. Put up a large poster-type calendar that changes monthly. Determine what calendar-related activities are developmentally appropriate for your students and what fits best into your curriculum. Then build a few calendar activities in your opening routines. Here are suggestions from Jewish teachers throughout the country.

1 *Hebrew language activities.* Use the calendar to teach Hebrew vocabulary: yesterday, today, tomorrow; days of the week, days of creation; question words: What day is it? When is ____?; past tense and future tense verbs—Yesterday we____. Today we_____. Tomorrow we will_____; weather words—hot, cold, rain, snow, sun.

2 *Birthday activities.* Iris Petroff displays a *"Yom Huledet Sameah"* (happy birthday) banner on the wall. With the banner are signs for each month with each child's Hebrew birthday listed under the appropriate month. At the beginning of each session her students use their classroom calendar to determine the English and Hebrew dates, then celebrate the birthdays that happen during the week.

3 *Rosh Hodesh activities.* Judy Miller's students become "official moon watchers." Students begin at the start of a given month and draw the shape of the moon each day. They can track how the phases change and correlate with Rosh Hodesh. Give each student his/her own calendar grid to take home and use for drawing the shape of the moon each evening. If it's too cloudy, they record that fact by drawing a cloud.

4 *Holiday activities.* Sukkot, Pesah and Shavuot all occur during the full moon, and they are all pilgrimage holidays. Why is the full moon important to these holidays? Compare and contrast the three *regalim* using the calendar activities as a springboard for the discussion. Use your classroom calendar to discuss and count the *omer*, to mark the number of days between holidays (a special indication for the ten days of awe), etc.

5 *Life cycle events.* Bunnie Piltch uses the Jewish calendar to foster awareness of life cycle events. Her students bring to class a list of dates (including exact year) that mark important events in their lives. She looks up the corresponding Hebrew dates. Students construct paper booklets with enough pages for a cover and one full page for each month. Each page includes the Hebrew name of the month as a heading, the names and dates of the holidays that occur in that month, and any of the life cycle events on the students' lists. Students design pop-ups or simple illustrations that pertain to the events listed for each month. The lunar principles of the calendar are taught to help students understand the logic of the holiday dates. Students can follow the sequence of the Jewish year from a personal perspective (bar/bar mitzvah, grandparent's yahrzeit) while learning the dates of the holidays.

Rosh ha-Shanah/Yom Kippur Activity:
Five Projects for Beginning the New Year

I could never separate the closing of one school year from preparation for the next. As each bulletin board was dismantled, old art projects "auctioned off" and textbooks sorted, I was thinking about how I'd do it differently next year.

Here are five projects to get you and your class ready for the new year.

1 *Work with your principal to create a school bulletin board to welcome students.* Sometime in August collect photographs of each teacher on the staff. Ask the teachers to write a New Year's wish—for the school, the congregation, the world, their class. Before school begins post the bulletin board in a high traffic area in the building.

2 *New class lists are usually ready in August.* As soon as you have access to your new class list, write a letter welcoming each student. (If you use a computer, choose an appropriate type size for the age of your students.) The letter should be a personal one, reflecting your personality and style, and should set the tone for the year. It may include upcoming highlights from the curriculum, instructions to bring something to class on the first day, or a question to consider. Invite the students to stop by the building, read the faculty's New Year's wishes, and try to match the teachers' names with their faces.

3 *Idie Benjamin focuses her opening discussion on old/new.* She brings to class a pile of ratty old clothes mixed with new ones. Students go through the pile comparing the garments. The discussion then turns to what's new in students' lives, such as shoes, clothes, classroom, teacher, friends, siblings, etc. Then on to Rosh ha-Shanah—a new <u>h</u>allah shape, a new sound (shofar), and most importantly new behavior to replace old, worn-out behavior. Idie (who teaches in a day school) also integrates these concepts across curriculum areas: science—transformations; nature—changing seasons; cognitive—new concepts, learning goals for the year.

4 *The central ritual and mitzvah of Rosh ha-Shanah is the blowing of the shofar.* Its "wake-up call" provides a great focus for activities and discussions at the beginning of the year. For example, older students can try to solve a mystery: Why do we blow the shofar on Rosh ha-Shanah? Leave a "clue" at each of four stations around the room. Divide the class into four groups that rotate through all four stations, reading and discussing the clues. Brainstorm and record students' theories. (The "clues" are four texts—*Yeshaya* (Isaiah) 27:13; *Bereshit* (Genesis) 22:13; *Shemot* (Exodus) 19:18,19; and the passage from the shofar service "This is the day, the beginning of creation, a remembrance of the first day."

5 *The High Holy Days are about vows and sins and promises and introspection.* Read "Rainbow People" from *God's Mailbox* by Marc Gellman. In this story God looks every day for one person who is doing good things. It's a wonderful springboard for discussions about our roles in finishing God's creation.

Five Great Hanukkah Party Ideas

The important thing about classroom parties is to make them meaningful—much more than candy, popcorn, and the kids' favorite music CDs from home.

Use the classroom party as an opportunity to review, analyze and synthesize the story of Hanukkah; learn how to fulfill the mitzvot; expand upon the "giving" aspect of the holiday; involve families (or other special guests—another class or residents of the local Jewish home for the aged); and have a good time.

1 *Create a party that centers on the culmination of your Hanukkah study.* Students have studied the real story of Hanukkah and can use their knowledge to write a play or puppet show (complete with costumes and sets) that retells the story' or a retelling of the story with the three different endings as described in Torah Aura's *BJL Hanukkah* (page 26). Older students may want to stage a debate between Hillel and Shammai about the proper way to light the hanukkiyah or a play that explains Hanukkah to non-Jewish school friends.

2 *Plan a party that involves students moving through four or five "centers."* Each center develops a Hanukkah concept or provides an opportunity for students to expand and enrich their thinking. Have an adult, teacher's aide or high school student available to facilitate each station. Ideas for centers: [a] read or listen to a book on tape, then follow up with a writing or language experience activity; [b] make latkes or *sufganiyot* that are eaten at the end of the day; [c] make dreidels and play the dreidel game (have the rules printed on cards and a bag of peanuts available); [d] make a gift for parents; [e] practice saying the blessings and lighting the hanukkiyah; [f] write Hanukkah riddles to ask the class during the party; [g] sing and illustrate a Hanukkah song; [h] write new verses to "I Have a Little Dreidel."

3 *Ask students to come dressed as their favorite character in the Hanukkah story or as one of the Jews or Syrians.* Cook and eat latkes, play the dreidel game and sing Hanukkah songs.

4 *Focus the party on creating gifts.* Some gift ideas: [a] Work with your local Jewish Family Service to find out what your class can do for needy Jewish families; [b] Dorothy Finsel's class is making beanbag Tic-Tac-Toe games for First Place, Seattle's school for homeless children.

5 *There are dozens of small new businesses that provide ceramics that you paint, glaze and fire.* I've learned that some of them will come to your school and provide clay dreidels to paint and glaze. There is a time factor (for firing the dreidel) and a cost. But a beautifully painted and glazed dreidel that every child takes home can become a family heirloom ritual item.

One more idea—plan a major family program. Invite the families to join your class. Three things to do with the families: (1) Adults and kids could go through a "centers" activity together; (2) Create a huge interactive game that everyone plays; (3) *BJL Hanukkah* (page 48) suggests dividing the whole group into five teams of families and assigning each family to write a three-minute play on one of the five following scenes: [a] Greeks show the Jews all the 'gifts they are bringing'; [b] an argument between Jews who want to do Greek things and Jews who want to do only Jewish things; [c] Antiochus ordering the Jews not to do Jewish things (and having his soldiers mess up the Temple); [d] Mattathias fighting back; and [e] Jews cleaning up the Temple and celebrating the first Hanukkah.

For a wonderful Hanukkah resource: *The Art of Jewish Living: Hanukkah* by Dr. Ron Wolfson.

Five Purim Activities for Your Classroom

When I was growing up we made crepe paper costumes every Purim and paraded through the halls of the temple. Fold the crepe paper in half; cut a hole for the head and a long rectangle for the sash. Decorate a crown. I can still feel and smell that crepe paper. I still remember the embarrassment I felt parading through the halls while the older kids stood outside their classroom doors and laughed. In the '50s, who knew about age-appropriate?

1 *Linda Kirsch's school does a two-hour Purim family program for fourth grade.*

[a] Small groups of six to eight adults and children sit in circles and read a Purim shpiel, reader's theatre style.

[b] A facilitator joins each group for a values-based discussion that includes talking about the mitzvot connected with Purim.

[c] Each person creates a megillah. The scrolls are already put together, and outlines of people are pre-drawn on each panel. Families find pictures in magazines to glue onto the megillah for costumes, animals, foliage, furniture, background.

[d] The program concludes with singing and hamantaschen.

2 *A neat high school idea from Paul Epstein.* CONCEPT: The Purim story features exaggerated portrayals of contemporary Jewish and secular leaders. One way to look at the text is as a humorous critique of the rulers of the day. Could Ahasuerus really have been so obtuse? Could Haman really have been so ironically evil and stupid? Who is this Mordecai, constantly plotting in the wings? IMPLEMENTATION: Read and discuss sections of the Purim text, emphasizing this concept. Examine contemporary political cartoons, drawing a comparison. The features are "larger than life," and the characters are extra-evil, extra-virtuous or extra-stupid. Students draw their own political cartoons.

3 *Life Masks.* Dan Bender sends a "two-fer." A great project and the best classroom management technique ever: life masks. Carapace (original formula) is a fast-setting plaster gauze, normally used to set broken bones. However, for making a life mask you cut the gauze into strips and place them on the Vaseline-covered face of a child who is lying on a table. It takes fifteen to twenty minutes for the plaster to harden. The student wiggles his nose, chin and forehead to break the mask free. Trim edges with scissors, cut eyeholes and a mouthpiece, and get ready to decorate with markers or poster paints.

4 *Laurie Hoffman makes groggers from 16-ounce clear water bottles.* Give each student a piece of paper that has been carefully measured and cut to fit around the bottle. Students cut pictures from magazines to create a collage of the Purim characters. When the collage is completed, roll the paper and slip it inside the bottle to expand against the side. Now you have a tzedakah box that serves as a grogger. Students can retell the Purim story by looking at the pictures.

5 *At Temple B'nai Torah the third grade class puts Haman and Mordecai on trial.* A parent/lawyer works with the class to develop questions that will help build cases for both prosecuting and defending Haman and Mordecai.

Ten Classroom Pesaḥ Projects

Here is a series of classroom projects that can be used in stations, as individual activities, or as part of family workshops. Create a Pesaḥ Learning Experience or Pesaḥ Happening that utilizes a series of activities that incorporates all the senses—art, writing, cooking, reading, singing. Here are ten classroom projects.

1 *Bring REAL horseradish and a recipe for making horseradish.* Students can taste and work with the real thing.

2 *Set up a station where students can make different kinds of ḥaroset* (traditional, Egyptian, Sephardic, Persian, Moroccan).

3 *Divide up the haggadah.* Assign each student (or group of students) some research about "their" section of the haggadah.

4 *Make pillows for leaning at the seder.* Students can embroider or paint on fabric.

5 *Students can make afikomen holders.* My colleagues in our Israel Program Center tell me that the April, 1997 issue of *Martha Stewart's Living* has some wonderful ideas.

6 *Teach your students how to make matzah and the laws about matzah making and baking.* All you need is flour, water, a timer and something with which to make holes. Rivy's father, when he lived in Russia, used the gears of a watch to make the holes.

7 *Help children write their own plays depicting the story of the Exodus* or a portion of the story—the burning bush, crossing the Sea of Reeds, the ten plagues, etc. Use *Sedra Scenes* as inspiration.

8 *Teach students how to make and use a chart for counting the omer.* Laminate the chart for multi-year use.

9 *Teach or review the order of the seder.* Cut out representative objects and/or names (kadesh, urḥatz, etc.), and laminate each piece. Affix a magnet or piece of Velcro to the back of each. Laminate a poster board and create a game or self-checking independent activity. For older students use Torah Aura's *Fifteen Steps to Freedom* to teach the structure of the seder.

10 *Hold a discussion about what it was like to leave Egypt.* Your students will probably be inspired to make their own video. You can use Torah Aura's *My Exodus* as a springboard for the conversation.

Seven More Pesah Projects

The holiday that takes the most preparation and work seems to generate class projects that take the most preparation and work. But if you're looking for new ways to deepen, extend, enrich and build upon the learning from last year, our "Five things" advisory group submitted some wonderful programs and activities.

1 *Retelling our stories.* Susan Fish faced the challenge of creating an interactive family Passover program without a model seder. She decided to focus on specific elements of the seder and to emphasize the message of "retelling our stories." The haggadah was the focus of the stations that were repeated in two classrooms. The children and their families were divided into groups and covered four different learning stations. The program began with a warm-up that asked families to pair up and tell a Passover family event they remembered. The families and their second graders then spent about an hour at the four stations, coming together at the end to sing a seder song and watch a slide show made by Jewish Day School second graders in 1990 titled "Exodus." The stations included the following: [a] "Play With the Plagues"—Hebrew vocabulary matching games, [b] "Four More Questions" to ask at the seder, [c] "The Three Symbols of Passover"—artistic collage related to freedom; and [d] "Dayenu—We Are Grateful for What God Has Given to the World"—research using magazines to locate words and/or pictures related to the song.

2 *Collecting haggadot.* Some students at Seattle's Community High School of Jewish Studies elected a class that spent the winter trimester in anticipation of Pesah. They studied the structure and content of the haggadah by examining diverse examples, then compiled their favorite translations of each section and wrote supplementary texts. Principal Paul Epstein suggests that even if you didn't start this project three months ago, it's still an interesting exercise to have students bring in a variety of haggadot to compare and contrast. If you have a large enough class you can assign one section to each pair of students, who could compile their own Haggadah supplement in two class sessions.

3 *Dessert seder.* In San Antonio Deena Bloomstone's congregation ends Passover with a dessert seder. Grade 2 parents prepare all the ritual food items for the table. Students prepare table decorations as well as a little musical that they present while everyone is eating. The rabbi conducts the seder, calling on participants to take turns with the English readings. Students from the Hebrew school present the Hebrew segments of the seder. When it comes to the meal, they have dessert! The dessert seder is held on the last evening of Passover, and the religious school families (as well as anyone else) are invited to attend. The sisterhood foots the bill for dessert.

4 *Two-week seder prep.* Linda Kirsch's fifth grade family program is a two-week affair. The first week families (in all the fifth grade classes) visit fifteen stations, one for each step in the seder. At each station is an activity geared to each step, including finding and burning ḥametz, hand washing, making an afikoman bag, discussing ten modern plagues. This first visit also includes an activity in which families make Passover cards for residents of the local Jewish senior citizen home. The second week is the family (by class) Seder, conducted by family participants.

5 *Family Education Day for grades 4–6.* Judy Podolsky's favorite Pesaḥ event includes five stations: [a] learning the seder melodies and receiving copies of the music to take home; [b] a matzah-making station that begins with the Torah Umesorah video on making matzah and is followed by mixing, rolling and baking the matzah; [c] a discussion in which parents and kids sit together to figure out the most essential things for them to take if they are running away and walking a long distance; [d] discussing the meaning of covenant: Families discuss what covenants they have in their families as part of their relationships. They then create a family banner on muslin with fabric paints and glue-on items that represent their covenantal relationship with one another; [e] a last station where families discuss the negatives and positives of slavery versus liberty, as well as the survival skills that free people need, ending with a discussion of why forty years in the desert. This family day concludes with singing the seder melodies together in the social hall.

6 Judy Miller suggests *an intergenerational seder with the retirement center in Tulsa.* Soliciting cooking help from parents, children make paper flowers and place cards for the table, and everyone has a part in the seder. The children gain immense respect for their elders, and the adults get a bird's-eye view of the great education their kids are getting. The bonus is that many of the children have grandparents who live far away, and many of the elderly have grandchildren out of town. This program gives both groups an opportunity to have a lovely intergenerational experience with someone close by.

7 *Through Partnership 2000 Judy's school has established a relationship with Kinneret Elementary in Israel.* During the first week in April their school will have a joint seder via satellite linkup. The local community college facilitated a linkup in December so both schools could light Ḥanukkah candles together. Tulsa children spoke in Hebrew. The Israeli children spoke in English. For the upcoming seder Judy has worked closely with their *shliḥah* (Israeli exchange leader), Anat Ha-Cohen, to develop a special haggadah for the program.

Five Ways to Help Your Students Enhance Their Sedarim

A dozen years ago my son Rob's teacher at the Jewish Day School sent home a simple letter that began:

"<u>H</u>ag Sameah. Enclosed in this week's folder are some ideas for your Seder...."

That packet of ideas forever changed the way we conduct our Seder. Beth Huppin is an extraordinary teacher. She knew whom she was teaching when she sent those Pesa<u>h</u> materials home—long before family education became a household word. This week I share with you five ideas you can send home with your students to enhance their home *Sedarim*.

1 *Rob's class wrote a first-person account of leaving Egypt.* He brought his "journal of a slave" home to read during the *maggid* (historical) section of the seder. You can develop any number of creative writing class projects for kids to take home. One year my sons and their friends did a rock musical that they taped for video viewing during the Seder.

2 *The Seder is a time for questions.* The four questions were originally only suggested questions for those who did not know what to ask. Have your students go through the haggadah and develop a question for each paragraph (or each section being studied). Give students the entire set of questions to take home for discussion during their Seder.

3 *Ask each student to bring a favorite Pesah recipe.* Create a class Pesa<u>h</u> cookbook for each family. Be sure someone includes a recipe for matzah almond roca. It gives a whole new meaning to matzah.

4 *Tape all the Passover songs your students are learning.* Send each student home with a copy of the tape to share with his/her family. A hint: The order of the Seder fits perfectly with the chorus of "Dayenu". (I've never been able to remember the traditional melody.)

5 *Include modern versions of the traditional.* On the Internet I found The Four Questions as they would have been written by Dr. Seuss (now found in most bookstores as *Uncle Eli's Haggadah*). In her life-changing send-home packet Beth included "The Ballad of the Four Sons" that is sung to the tune of "My Darling Clementine". *The Women's Haggadah* includes "The Song of Questions" by E.M. Broner and Naomi Nimrod. Some years ago the National Jewish Resource Center published "The Fifth Child" (a child of the *Shoah* [Holocaust]) to be inserted in the Seder before opening the door for Elijah.

And of course you can send articles or stories from your own collection and Seder. Beth sent Danny Siegel's "My Father's Personal Passover Ritual," a moving piece we still read at our Seder that brings another understanding to the meaning of freedom. "At the Waters of Meribah: A midrash for Pesah" by Marc Gellman and "Who Owns Our Time?" by Rabbi Harold Kushner offer two other ways to think about freedom. Beth Huppin is now my teacher. She is also a colleague and friend. I know a good thing when I see it.

Five Pesah Activities for the Early Childhood Classroom

Pesah. It's so much work. And so much challenge. Especially when it comes to making complicated concepts meaningful to young children. Here are five strategies for teaching Pesah concepts in the early childhood and kindergarten classroom. With thanks to Idie Benjamin, Laurel Abrams, and Rabbi Elana Zaiman.

1 *First talk about bread.* Then talk about matzah. Write recipes for both on large chart paper. First the class makes hallah from scratch (a several-hour project). On another day students make matzah. Students can then compare the making of bread to the making of matzah—the number of ingredients, the number of steps involved, and the time it takes to make each. (A beautiful math lesson, too.)

2 *Leaving Egypt.* In the middle of an engrossing project, stop all activity and announce that it's time to go. What do we have to do? Pack!!!! What do we bring? (A couple of kids made sure to bring their dolls.) Everyone scurries to pack. Or create a chart listing what students would take if they had to leave their homes quickly—a great language experience activity. March out of the room—don't forget to split the sea somewhere.

3 *Teaching haroset.* Demonstrate the importance of cement. Use small blocks of wood, styrofoam, or other scrap (recycled) materials. Stack them up; give a push. It all falls down. Now build the stack with a thick layer of glue between each piece. Touch and it still stands. If your school is made of cinder blocks, show students the mortar lines between the blocks and/or point out the grout lines between the tiles in the bathroom.

4 *Tears.* What brings tears to your eyes? Tell about a time you cried. What made you cry? Did you ever taste your tears? What did they taste like? Create tears by mixing salt and water. Do you feel better when you cry?

Peel and slice a real horseradish. What happens when you taste it? Did it make you sweat? Bring in other bitter foods (endive, etc). Describe the tastes. Then ask questions about being comforted. When you're crying, what makes you feel better? What comforts you? By tasting and eating we're remembering—we move from tears to smiles.

5 *Questions and stories.* Plan your class Seder with questions in mind—begin with dessert—do things differently so students will ask, "what's going on here?" The whole notion of the Seder is to ask questions and to tell stories. What stories does the matzah tell? What stories do we learn from each of the foods on the seder plate?

Classrooms can foreshadow what we hope will happen in our students' homes. Our tradition tells us to be prepared to answer our children's questions. Hopefully, these classroom activities will generate dozens of questions for the Seder at home.

Five (Really Eleven) Pesaḥ Ideas for Home and School (or from School to Home)

There is never a dearth of Pesaḥ ideas, projects, activities, recipes. Here are some interesting ones I received this past week.

1 *Walk-on Seder plate.* To help young students understand the meaning of the Pesaḥ symbols, Leora Zeitlin created a HUGE seder plate on which students constructed graphic representations of the seder symbols (as opposed to the symbols themselves). Once the construction appeared on the plate it was easy to replace it with the symbol itself. For *ḥaroset*—styrofoam bricks glued together; *maror*—a construction of our people building pyramids; for the *z'roa*—a mezuzah on a doorway; for the *baytzah*—the "rebirth"—a construction of Sinai and receiving the Torah.

2 *Movable feast.* Rabbi Jerry Kane creates a seder with a nomadic flavor. The seder begins informally with "hors d'oeuvres and drinks" and guests standing around the table in the dining room. Candles are lit, kiddush is sung, *karpas* is dipped. Guests then wander into the living room and find a comfortable place, taking cups to sip wine while talking through the *maggid*. "More than four questions" are asked, followed by a variety of special readings. The next move is to another "dining area" for the meal and accompanying rituals (*matzah, maror, korekh*). Finally guests return to the lounging area for *tzafun, birkat ha-mazon*, more singing and the conclusion.

3 *Living time-line.* An activity for sixth graders that integrates Pesaḥ, history, text. Dan Bender's students look at the Talmud (*Pesaḥim* 116b, "*Arvei Pesaḥim*") and compare it to the traditional Haggadah's mention of *pesaḥ/matzah/maror*. Their texts are *Understanding Jewish History*, pp.110-113; *Jewish History*, printed by Tzvi and Elkie Black; and *Toldot Am Olam*, by Sholomo Rottenberg, to make certain that students understand the historical implications of "In every generation, each person is required to see herself as if she had come out from slavery in Egypt" (*Talmud Pesaḥim* 116b after *Pesaḥ, matzah, maror*).

First students read the English translation of "Pesaḥ" from the Shottenstein translation of the Talmud, then the English of the haggadah. Then "Matzah", in both places, then "Maror" from both the Talmud translation and the haggadah. Students conclude that the two texts are virtually identical. Next, students go to the Jewish history time-line. One student stands at Y2K looking back (to the left) toward a student at 200 C.E. (Mishnah), and a third student stands on the far left at 1500 B.C.E.. The student in the middle speaks to the student in present time (Y2K) and explains to him his obligation to experience the Seder as a personal exodus from Egypt with the student standing back at 1500 B.C.E. (behind him). Students are able to place the Exodus, the Talmud, and Y2K in their proper relation, cover the Hebrew and English reading of the haggadah, explore traditional Jewish texts, and experience with their bodies the relationship of historical events.

4 *You are there.* One person is assigned to be the reporter. Others pick a role out of a hat. Offer a wide range of roles—Pharaoh, Jewish child, Jewish slave, average Egyptian citizen, frog, wild beast, Miriam, Aaron, etc. The reporter asks each character a question about his or her experience and perceptions. This activity has a wide grade-level appeal and also works well as a take home experience to enhance home Sedarim.

5 *In the bag.* Students create ritual and creative items to use at their family Sedarim.

[a] **Steps of the Seder booklet:** Cut fifteen footprints for pages. On each "page" write (in English or Hebrew or both) and illustrate one of the steps of the Seder. Punch a hole in the heels and attach a brad.

[b] **Four cups:** Using clear plastic wine cups and permanent markers, have students create their own four cups. Have them number the cups and decorate each.

[c] **Seder plate:** Students draw or color the seder symbols. Cut them out and tape the symbols to the top of a clear plastic plate. Then place another clear plastic plate on top. The top plate can be filled and washed for reuse. The pictures on the bottom plate will stay dry and clean.

[d] **Elijah's cup:** Create a beautiful Elijah's cup by using a foil covering on two paper or styrofoam cups glued bottom to bottom. You can also send home Elijah stories to be read during the Seder.

[e] **Songs for the Seder**: Include copies of fun songs for the Seder. The old "Ballad of the Four Sons," sung to the tune of "Clementine" is still fun. This week I received e-mail with seder words to "There's No Business Like Show Business," "Maria," (from *West Side Story*), "Just a Spoonful of Sugar," and "Do You Hear the People Sing" (from *Les Miserables*).

[f] **Plagues in a bag:** Ask students to search their homes and novelty stores to find tiny plastic locusts, cows, and other toys that will serve as boils, hail, babies, frogs. I use a tiny bottle of red water for the blood, but a red scarf or red tissue paper is good. If all else fails you can buy plagues in a bag at Archie McPhee's <www.mcphee.com>

[g] **Afikomen bag:** Use muslin for the bag (or you could use a manila envelope). To create a really neat textured matzah-like pattern, use a piece of ¼-inch hardware cloth (it looks like tightly woven chicken wire). Place the hardware cloth under the muslin. Use the side of a brown crayon and rub.

Place all the items in a large decorated shopping bag for ease of transporting to sedarim!

Five Prince of Egypt Study Guides

1 *<prince-of-egypt.com>* (a guide for the effective use of the film by Rabbi Elliot Dorff)

2 *<bjesf.org/familyeducation>* (companion materials by Vicky Kelman for adults who see the movie with children)

3 *<libertynet.org/acaje/ftorah.html>* (Family Time for Torah: Exodus, an ACAJE publication)

4 *"Let My People Go to the Movies,"* a 16-page booklet published by the JCC of Chicago

5 *"Exodus Study Guide"* from the Jewish Education Services Department of Jewish Community Federation, Rochester, N.Y.

(Thanks to Nancy Messinger, who forwarded this information from HASAFRAN, the Association of Jewish Libraries.)

Seven Ways (and Many Resources) to Help Commemorate Yom ha-Shoah

"...[T]he few human survivors of the Holocaust...have an important task now. To build a new life...to remember what the world was like before so much was destroyed by evil...to repeat their memories...to tell their story to all who will listen" (from *The Promise of a New Spring*).

Teaching about the Holocaust and preparing for meaningful commemoration takes thoughtful planning. What follows are resources and project ideas to help.

1 Books: These books (with grade levels in parentheses), recommended by our advisory group, can serve as springboards for discussion, art and writing projects: *Escape from the Holocaust, The Terrible Things, Number the Stars* (4th–5th); *The Promise of a New Spring* (2nd–4th), *The Tattooed Torah* (3rd), *The Number on My Grandfather's Arm* (4th), *The Yanov Torah* (5th), *A Knock at the Door* (5th), *Anne Frank Remembered* (7th), *The Grey Striped Shirt* (2rd–4th).

2 Film: The video "*Journey of the Butterfly*." The American Boys Choir sings Pavel Freidman's poem, "I Never Saw Another Butterfly. " It is a moving musical rendition, beautifully done, recommended for seventh grade and up (and good with parents). Two excellent films that won 1998 Oscars are *The Long Road Home* and *Visas and Virtues*, both for older students.

3 The Internet: You will find a great deal of information and sources for appropriate projects on the Internet. Students can "visit" Yad Vashem <www.yad-vashem.org.il>, the United States Holocaust Memorial Museum <www.ushmm.org>, and The Museum of Tolerance <www.wiesenthal.com/mot>. Check out the Holocaust resources at the Bureau of Jewish Education in San Francisco <www.slip.net/~bjesf/resources.397>, where you will find an entire section on teaching the Holocaust and dozens of book and video suggestions.

4 Writing: Writing can be a very meaningful way for children to express their thoughts and feelings. Create a class book of original writing inspired by "I Never Saw Another Butterfly." Or provide one poem for each child to illustrate. Make a color copy of the work to make a full set of the poems, with illustrations by their classmates, for students to take home. On the San Francisco BJE website you will find a student project entitled "How My Family Survived" by Alisa Roberts, which will inspire your own research and writing projects.

5 Class projects:

[a] As part of their Yom ha-Shoah activities, students in Tina Rappaport's school repaired prayerbooks that had broken bindings. Inside the repaired siddurim they prepared and affixed a label that read "This prayerbook was respectfully repaired by (their name and age) in memory of (the name of a child who perished in the Holocaust—age, year, town). Information was provided by B'nai B'rith.

[b] Judy Podolsky suggests a project in which students design a yahrzeit plaque to commemorate the six million. The plaque is placed on the synagogue wall with the other yahrzeit plaques with a ceremony that is part of the synagogue's Yom ha-Shoah service.

[c] As recognition of the importance of graves and dates of death, students can develop a cemetery project. Students go out to a congregation or community cemetery to look at and clean up graves and set flowers. Students can also read the headstones to create a name and date registry for the congregation if no registry exists.

6 *The "Jewish Education News" (CAJE, Spring 1996) focuses on Holocaust education.* It is an excellent compilation of relevant articles and includes a survey of print resources.

7 *Torah Aura has three outstanding Instant Lessons* for sixth graders to adult: [a] a lesson on *Schindler's List* that contrasts the movie with the book; [b] "Trouble in Jewish Cheyenne," a lesson that allows students and teachers to confront anti-Semitism outside the pressure of a crisis situation; and [c] "What if the Fiddler Stopped Fiddling?," a lesson based on the film *Fiddler on the Roof* that explores different responses to anti-Semitism.

"...for you are the new spring in the forest of the world."

Five (Plus One) Projects for Yom Ha-Atzma'ut

Yom ha-Atzma'ut provides opportunities for teaching about Israel. The following projects are pieces of large school or community celebrations. Each piece can be adapted for your own classroom.

Marla Gamoran describes two projects at her children's elementary school in Jerusalem.

1 *At the entrance to the building the fictional Yisraeli family's home is set up like the first homes in the Yishuv.* Throughout the year the display changes to show how this early pioneering family celebrates each holiday. She says, "It's been fun to see the changing of the year marked by holidays and Jewish traditions as a 1948 Israeli family would celebrate and live."

2 *The Kitah B class has centers set up in the hallway that include kits/activities relating to the history of Zionism and the country for the children to do alone or in small groups.* A series of laminated cards contains information about various Israeli/Zionist leaders such as David Ben Gurion, Golda Meir, Theodore Herzl, etc. One side of each card contains some factual information about the person or event. The other side lists activities and questions relating to that person or event.

3 *Judy Miller's fourth and fifth grade students integrated their emphasis on tikkun olam with their study of Jerusalem.* They built a model of Jerusalem using all recycled materials. The finished project was 10'x12'. They used old soda cans stacked 2' high for the wall and sprayed them with "stone"-textured paint. The gates and buildings were made from old boxes, papier mâché and a "L'eggs" hosiery package wrapped in old lace ribbon and spray-painted to create the Dome of the Rock. The students labeled all the buildings and gates and then wrote a brief explanation of each structure's significance on cards that they glued to the rooftops.

4 *Make a class quilt to celebrate Israel.* Each child creates a quilt square depicting his/her feelings about Israel or some historic event that has been studied. If fabric is used, the squares are sewn together. Or use white paper and markers. To put the squares together like a quilt, use strips of construction paper between the squares backing the "quilt" with poster board or heavy butcher paper. Sue Brodsky Littauer's class put their quilt on the Internet with the assistance of their temple men's club. Each child's picture was taken. The individual photos and the quilt were scanned onto the mens' club web page.

Drora Arussy was the educational coordinator for "Israel at Fifty" in the San Francisco Bay area. At the suggestion of Debbie Findling she contributed the following fabulous projects:

5 *Structure a family education day during which families spend the day preparing for a birthday party.* Families all get involved in the party preparations while learning about various aspects of Israel. Stations are set up in classrooms to encourage families to learn about geography, food, music, etc. Stations can include:

[a] **Geography:** A room is filled with brochures, teachers in roles from various regions in Israel, topography maps, weather-related cutouts, etc. The family as a whole explores the various regions and chooses one to represent. They then create a backdrop of that region with each family member contributing at his or her own level. Presto—party decorations!

[b] **Food:** Names of various Israeli specialties are hung around a room in Hebrew and English. Families are encouraged to prepare food and taste it while learning the history and Hebrew names of the various ingredients. Presto—party munchies!

[c] **Music:** Either prepare family music videos or teach basic Israeli dance steps. A band, great food, decorations and the pride of seeing what they've done make this a personal celebration of Israel's independence. Presto—Party entertainment.

6 *Here is Drora's description of the Bay Area's Declaration of Independence project.* This outstanding project could be adapted and used for a class family education day—The Israel Declaration of Independence Project.

Families will embark on a mission to interpret the Declaration of Independence for a modern State of Israel. Stations will represent key variables and quotes from each section of the Declaration. At each station families will participate in an activity that results in the creation of a puzzle piece that will be used at the end of the project. The stations are:

[a] **Birthplace of the Jewish people & the Bible:** Tape recorders will be set up in which forefathers/foremothers will discuss their personal connection to the land of Israel. Families will be asked to listen to one or two of the recordings, briefly write a family Bible describing their connection to the State of Israel, and attach it as a scroll to the designated puzzle piece.

[b] **Holocaust reflection:** In one corner of the room there will be a black display with multiple copies of pictures and quotes about human suffering and strength during the Holocaust. Families will be asked to choose one to five of these copies and attach them to the designated puzzle piece.

[c] Pray and hope for return: A *bimah*, set up toward the middle of the room, will display texts of various prayers denoting yearning for the Jewish homeland. Families will read through the quotes and choose one prayer that they best relate to, or they can write their own prayer of longing for the Jewish State. This will be the next puzzle piece.

[d] **Immigration of all Jews:** A *tallit* will be suspended with verses related to the ingathering of Jews from the four corners of the earth and pictures of various *aliyot* attached. Under the *tallit* a table will be set up with papers of many colors. All the families at this booth will be asked to design a puzzle piece together that represents ingathering. Note: It is very important that working together be stressed, as input from various groups (i.e., families) is one of the foundations of the democratic State of Israel.

[e] **Call for peace:** A model of a dove will be suspended. Under it will be a table with Jewish and Israeli symbols and personalities, together with playing pieces and blocks. Families will be asked to develop a sculpture that symbolizes peace. Families will be encouraged to use human subjects as well as materials provided at the station. These sculptures will then be photographed with a Polaroid camera to create the next puzzle piece.

Upon completion of the entire odyssey families will be asked to assemble their puzzles, resulting in an outline of the modern state of Israel. This puzzle will also represent the personal, intellectual analysis that the family has undergone. These puzzles will be glued onto half a sheet of tag board. Family members who are present will be asked to sign their family interpretation of the Declaration of Independence. On the other half of the tag board families will attach a copy of the original text of the Declaration of Independence.

Forty Ways to Enrich the Teacher in You

Interviewing: Five Types of Questions Principals Should Ask Teachers

Spring is the time of year when some people are thinking about baseball. Jewish educators are thinking about winding down the school year, testing, report cards, picnics, assemblies, and rounding up missing library books. At the same time, Jewish educators are thinking about staffing for the next school year.

The résumés are on your desk. The *kitah gimmel* candidate is coming tomorrow. How can you learn as much as possible about his/her personal beliefs, Jewish background, teaching and management style, and potential working relationship with you?

1 *Teaching and management style*

Describe a classroom success.

Describe a classroom situation that was difficult for you. How did you handle it? What would you do differently?

If I were to watch your classroom with the sound turned off, what would I see?

Tell me about a great teacher you had. Is there a teacher you hope to emulate? In what ways?

What makes you a good teacher?

2 *Supervision*

What do you most want from a supervisor?

What kinds of feedback are most helpful to you? What kinds are least helpful?

Describe the perfect supervisor. What if I don't live up to it?

What does excellence look like to you? How can I support you in realizing it?

If we were looking to customize a workshop for you, what would that workshop look like?

3 *Working with students*

With what kind of student do you work best? What age group is your favorite?

What type of student is most challenging?

What is your greatest strength?

4. Personal beliefs and style

What is it about Judaism that most excites you?

With what Jewish issues or questions do you wrestle? What most concerns you?

What is it about Judaism that you want to transmit to your students? How do you do that?

What kinds of things do you like to read? What have you read recently that you'd recommend, and why?

What's your favorite part of the Torah, and why?

If you could ask God one question, what would it be? What do you think God would answer?

What was your Jewish education like? What aspects would you like your students to experience? What would you do differently?

Who are your Jewish role models?

5. The final questions

Is there anything I didn't ask you that I should have asked you?

What questions would you like to ask me?

Five Considerations When Interviewing for a Jewish Teaching Position

Sometimes signing a teaching contract is like marrying someone you've known for two hours. Whether you are a new teacher or an experienced one, the interview process is often the only opportunity you will have to learn about the school, its culture and the person who may become your supervisor/mentor.

1 *Send a résumé in advance of the interview.* If you've never written a résumé, there are many "how to" books available. No longer just chronologies of educational and work history, résumés can have formats that build on your skills and experiences outside the field of Jewish education. Include a cover letter, no longer than a page, that articulately talks about your goals.

2 *Prepare for your interview.*

[a] Dress professionally.

[b] Bring your résumé (even if you sent one in advance).

[c] Prepare a portfolio that contains photographs, documents, letters and examples of student work and projects that tell about you as a Jewish teacher.

3 *Think about the questions you may be asked and what your responses might be.*

4 *Be prepared with your own written questions.* In addition to giving the message that you put a lot of thought into the interview, there are things about the school you need to know. The following questions address issues of school philosophy, culture, supervision, professional development, and discipline:

Tell me about the culture of your school.

What is the school's philosophy about teaching Hebrew? Bible? God? Wearing *kippot*?

How do you handle discipline problems?

What do you look for in choosing teachers for your school?

Is there an orientation for new teachers?

What kinds of school and communal resources are available to teachers?

Are there opportunities for me to grow professionally?

How long have you been the principal here? Will you be here next year?

What percentage of teachers is returning faculty?

If I do something wrong in class, how will I hear about it?

If a parent calls you to complain about something that happened in my class, what will you do?

What are the rewards and challenges of teaching here?

5 *Send a note two or three days following the interview.* Thank the principal for his/her time, comment on an interesting aspect of your discussion, and express your continued interest in the position or inform the principal that you have accepted another position.

Five Books Recommended by Teachers for Teachers

Summer may not mean "vacation" to people who must hire faculty, order books, and prepare curriculum. Thinking that the summer might offer some leisure time, I called several Seattle area educators and asked them what books they would recommend for educators to read. Not one Judith Krantz or John Grisham.

1 Maria Erlitz, vice-principal of The Jewish Day School, recommends *Punished by Rewards* by Alfie Kohn, about what we get when we give incentives—a short term result buys a long-term negative.

Two people suggested books by Mary Pipher:

2 Debby Kerdeman, associate professor of education at the University of Washington, is reading *Reviving Ophelia*, about the pain of teenage girls. Debby says "It's alarming without being alarmist" and explores the importance of family, community and religious life during this period of spiritual ennui.

3 Joanne Glosser, educator at Herzl Ner Tamid, recommends *The Shelter of Each Other: Rebuilding Our Families*, in which Pipher explores how our culture contributes to the erosion of our families. A local reviewer described "reflections about how our culture socializes kids to withdraw from their families, and how modern psychology finds abnormality in love, duty, and caring."

4 How many of us have enjoyed someone's hospitality and then, on the drive home, trashed the hosts? Rivy Poupko Kletenik, Jewish Education Council colleague and Seattle Hebrew Academy teacher, just finished Joseph Telushkin's *Words That Hurt, Words That Heal,* which "sensitizes us to the power of words and advocates concrete ways to incorporate values into our everyday lives."

5 My recommendation? *Teaching with Love and Logic,* by Jim Fay and David Funk. This approach puts its arms around everything I believe about working with kids. Dignity is at the core of the student-teacher relationship. Jim Fay's techniques teach us how to be in control and avoid power struggles while teaching kids to take responsibility and think for themselves. (Great strategies for adult relationships, too.)

Three Sets of Five Great and Small Things You Can Do to Honor Your Teachers

We're always looking for meaningful ways to honor our teachers. Typically this is done at the end of the school year at a dinner, service, or "teacher appreciation day." This week's column addresses these culminating events and suggests some long term strategies to plan now and implement next year.

Five texts to use as themes for honoring teachers:

1 There is no higher honor than that which is due the teacher (*Mishneh Torah, Laws of Torah Study* 5:1).

2 Happy is the generation in which the great listen to the small, for then it follows obviously that in such a generation the small will listen to the great (*Rosh ha-Shanah 25b*).

3 What we need more than anything else is not textbooks but text people. It is the personality of the teacher that is the text that the pupils read; the text they will never forget (Rabbi Abraham Joshua Heschel).

4 Whoever teaches Torah to someone else's child—it's as if you have given birth to that child (Sanhedrin 19b).

5 Any sage who does not rise in the presence of his or her Master teacher is considered wicked, and will not live long, and will forget the Torah he or she has learned (Kiddushin 33b).

Five gift ideas:

1 *Gift certificates from a bookstore.*

2 *A recently published book*

3 *A CAJE membership*

4 *Tickets to a concert, ballet, opera, ballgame*

5 *A subscription to a Jewish or educational magazine*

Five ways to honor teachers all year round:

1 *Work with your school and synagogue boards to provide every teacher with a free congregational membership.*

2 *Give all teachers a special aliyah on Simḥat Torah.*

3 *Arrange for tuition vouchers for teachers' children to attend camp or religious or day school.*

4 *Make it your business to insure that every teacher has invitations for Shabbat and holiday meals.*

5 *Create a coupon book for teachers that includes such no cost but exciting items as "Shabbat Dinner at the Zeidmans," "An afternoon on the Mahrer's sailboat," "A walk around Greenlake with Rabbi Dov," etc.*

Five Things an Education Director Should Do Over the Summer

Rabbi Susie Heneson Moskowitz asked for a list of activities an educator should do over the summer to help the year go smoothly. Deena shared her list last week—now here is mine. We know that summer means cleaning files, ordering textbooks and materials, creating forms, updating teacher/parent handbooks, and hiring faculty. Let's move on from there.

1 *In creating your own calendar be sure to include the school or synagogue's budget cycle* as well as that of the Federation or any Foundation to which you are planning to write a grant. Work backward from these deadlines. Planning must start now so the political work/lobbying can take place long in advance of the deadline for submitting budgets and proposals.

2 *Start building a strong school board.* Meet with the chair. Together, determine goals for the year, who will be asked to serve on the board, dates for meetings. Develop an action plan for moving your agenda forward. Refer to the time-line addressed above.

3 *Meet with each teacher individually.* (At a second meeting you may want to meet with teams of teachers.) Talk about school and individual goals and expectations for the year. Go through the curriculum and calendar. Talk about what's been successful in the past and what needs to be worked on for next year.

4 *Meet with every new school family.* Learn as much as you can about them and their children. Talk about school goals. Promote your vision and agenda. Plant seeds about adult and family learning opportunities; the importance of continuing Jewish education beyond bar/bat mitzvah; camp, Israel, and youth group during the high school years.

5 *Dream.* Vision. Talk about goals for the year—the kind of dreaming you don't have time to do when you're "fire-fighting." Plan things for yourself that you know you won't have time to do during the year. Go to a conference. Buy tickets to plays, concerts, sporting events. Consider buying season tickets, which will force you to set aside time for yourself.

Five Things You Can Do to Enrich Yourself Over the Summer

The previous chapter focused on activities that educators can engage in to prepare for the next school year. There were five useful, planful, classroom-related, pro-active ideas. In this chapter I'd like to recommend that you think about yourself. Steven Covey calls it "sharpening the saw." It's about taking care of you. Unless you get yourself well oiled you won't be useful to anyone—students, family, yourself. It's more than burnout prevention. It's about enriching yourself spiritually, intellectually, physically, socially.

1 *Take classes.* Switch roles. Instead of providing education, become a learner. Check out the wide variety of summer classes that are offered through universities, extension courses, public park systems. Go national. Consider the UAHC Kallah, Eilat Chayim, the National Chavurah conference, programs offered by the University of Judaism, the CAJE conference.

2 *Take trips.* In-town field trips to browse around a local teacher store. If you're taking travel plans, take some time to learn about the Jewish community in the town where you'll be vacationing. Depending on what you find, you may want to bring back slides to share with your class. You may also want to check out Jewish book and gift stores as well as Jewish resource centers and libraries.

3 *Read.* Read the books you didn't have time to read during the school year. Rivy has two personal reading projects. Every summer she tries to read three classics. Last year it was Dickens, Dostoevsky, and Austen. One summer she read the entire Tanakh. At the conclusion of each chapter she wrote, in a notebook, one summarizing sentence. This project could take five summers. It might also motivate you to study throughout the year.

4 *Find a new website.* Paul suggests <www.amazon.com>. Here you will find dozens of book reviews and lists. Books you must read. Books you should read. Just a click will get you to a list of Pulitzer prize winning books or books by Nobel winners. Once a month The Editors' series is listed—lists on many topics. Click on EYES. Type in a key word—a subject, topic, or theme that interests you—and EYES will do a word search. The list will automatically be e-mailed to you as new books are released in those areas.

5 *Exercise.* Teachers rarely take time during the school year to walk, jog, pump iron, watch what they eat. Summer is a time to look after your physical self, too. Make a commitment to do at least one type of exercise on a regular basis.

Take good care of yourself. You'll be ready to stare down September with a renewed outlook.

Forty-one Things About Using Torah Aura Materials

Six Ways to Use Bim Bam and C. Ha

Bim Bam and *C. Ha* are two-page newsletters that are faxed weekly to schools. They are perfect tools for building ten-minute learning opportunities. They're meaningful, they're topical, and they lend themselves to generic as well as specific student-directed independent activities. If you choose, there need be no preparation on the part of the teacher. Someone else did the work.

C. Ha is designed for fifth, sixth and seventh graders. *Bim Bam* is designed for high school students. Depending on your class and your goals, either of these publications can be used with seventh and eighth graders. Here are six ways to use these newsletters in your classroom.

A prerequisite: Be sure there is a map of the Middle East prominently displayed in the classroom with a box of push pins and/or Post-it notes nearby so kids can pinpoint where events are happening. Mark the places that make the news every week.

1 *Make a set of generic task cards.* Each week students come into class and take a newsletter and a task card. Find a partner and go to work. Examples of task cards:

[a] Choose the news item that is the most interesting (amazing, shocking) and summarize: who, what, when, where, why, implications.

[b] Choose one article. Explain why you chose it and what you learned.

[c] Develop the Room 12 Book of Lists. Keep separate, ongoing lists for personalities, issues, events, values, places. One task card will ask students to add to each list.

[d] Take three small pieces of paper. On each write one question based on this week's newsletter, with the answer on the back. Put the questions in the classroom quiz box. These questions can be pulled out and answered during transitions or at the end of the day. Toward the end of the year the questions can be compiled into a Trivial Pursuit or College Bowl-type game.

2 *Create a classroom encyclopedia* (or glossary) based on the personalities (Arafat, King Hussein, Ezer Weizman, Madeleine Albright), issues (k'lal Yisrael, who is a Jew, doctor-assisted suicide, organ donation), places (Old City, Har Homa, West Bank, Hebron), and institutions (the alphabet of Jewish life—WZO, ARZA, UJA, UN, IDF—location, purpose, how it affects us) discussed in each issue.

3 *Time-lines.* Choose a topic to follow—e.g., the peace process. Students read and summarize the articles in one sentence on a Post-it note and stick it on the wall, thereby creating a visual sequence of events.

4 C. _Ha has a weekly Torah moment._ Ask students to write a sentence or talk with a friend about the Torah message; e.g., (from C. _Ha_ 2.25), "Why do you think the Torah calls Israel the land of Milk and Honey?"

5 _Get involved in the discussion._ Both publications invite reader involvement and an interchange of ideas. Have students submit letters to the editor. Choose one student to submit responses on behalf of the class.

6 _A bonus idea!_ Bring in the week's worth of daily papers. Ask students to choose a new item from _Bim Bam_ or C. _Ha_. Then locate the more detailed article in the city paper.

Make _Bim Bam_ and C. _Ha_ a habit. When students come in the door, direct them to choose one of the activities to complete (with or without a partner). Another option is to discuss one of the hot topics during the opening routine.

A culminating activity for the end of the year: Choose the most important Jewish news story of the year. The class works together to determine the criteria, and to review and nominate. Students may be chosen to make a case for the story that most interests them. Then the class votes.

Let's be honest. We teachers are so busy that we may not be able to keep up on the news ourselves. Providing our students with _Bim Bam_ and C. _Ha_ opportunities sharpens their thinking and analytical skills, encourages them to keep abreast of the news, and gives them a Jewish news background on which to build.

Five Ways to Use Now I Know My Alef-Bet

1 *Big books:* Create a big book dictionary—either one dictionary for the entire class or one for each student. Allow students to add a description (with the help of the teacher or *madrikh/madrikhah*) and a drawing. Make a big book story with Hebrew words. Or reinforce the vocabulary from the celebration lesson, such as "In my *mish-pahah*, there is an *abba, imma, saba, savta,* etc."

2 *Create a running list of vocabulary and names.* Every time you get to a new word, add it to your running list. It can be vertical or horizontal.

3 *On a board, trace the Hebrew letters of your students' Hebrew names.* When you get to a new letter, any child with that letter in his or her name can decorate the letter, or put up a cutout of the letter on construction paper.

4 *If available, use the sandbox in the play area to let students trace letters in the sand.* Make Hebrew letters out of clay (try Crayola Model Magic), paint them, and display or put in a treasure box.

5 *Sing Debbie Friedman's "Alef-Bet Song."* Use it to set the tone, heighten expectation, build excitement or review the lesson. Create an alef-bet wall chart that is color coded to the song (*alef, bet, vet* in blue, *gimmel, dalet, hey* in green, etc.).

Five Ways to Use the Alef Celebrations Lessons

1 *Stations:* Break up some of the work into stations.

2 *Make a calendar or a year cycle device.* Each day your class can look to see where they are in the year and what celebrations are upcoming. Add your students' birthdays so that they know when they are in relationship to the celebrations.

3 *If your room is your own, make a student-sized Beit K'nesset.* If you have an especially creative nature, or a volunteer parent, create your wall out of foam core or corrugated cardboard. Add the *aron ha-kodesh, ner tamid,* and all the other items found in the Beit K'nesset—Torah, siddurim, *kippot* and *tallitot,* for example. Then create places for non-Beit K'nesset props to go.

4 *Make stuffed objects of holiday and Beit K'nesset items* (etrog, shabbat candle sticks, shofar, etc.). Place them in a drawer or box. When you need the lulav, you will have the lulav.

5 *Big books:* Make a big book story. You can create a story about a holiday celebration of something found in the Beit K'nesset. You can personalize the story to your class by leaving blanks and taking suggestions on how to fill them, or letting your students write the story. You can also make a book in the shape of your story's subject. Just think about the story "Sammy the Shofar" in the shape of the shofar (see "Make a Big Book" in *Five Great Classroom Book Projects,* pages 113-114 for ideas.)

Five Ways to Use the Posters for
Now I Know My Alef Bet and
Marilyn Price & Friends Present the Alphabet
from Alef to Tav

1 *Introduce the words for the week.* Show the key word and say "This is *karpas*. We eat karpas on Passover. *Karpas* begins with a *kaf*. It sounds like a 'k.' Can you hear the sound of the *kaf* in the word *karpas*? Listen again. *Karpas, kaf*. Do you hear it now? *Karpas, kaf*. Proceed with other *kaf* words reviewing as you go.

2 *Pin up on a clothesline some of the mini-posters of new words and those you have already learned.* Ask students to name them. Give each student a Hebrew letter. When you point to a poster, ask the student holding that letter to stand. After they have done a few, have students cover their eyes and take away one of the pictures. Ask students to name the word that is gone. Reverse the process and add a word. The same thing can be achieved if you lean mini-posters against the chalk board.

3 *Play a game.* Group students in teams. Show a member of one team a word and ask that child to say what the word (or the letter it begins with) is. Then show a card to a member of the second team. Or allow the teams to show the cards to each other. You can be the judge and point keeper.

4 *Use the mini-posters to review the celebration lessons.* Ask students to choose all the words used for Sukkot. Or find all the things that belong in the Beit K'nesset. Pass out the cards you have learned and ask students to stand in groups that belong together. Or call out a category: "Everyone who is holding a card of something that grows, stand up."

5 *Review.* Say "Do you remember this word? It begins with a _____. It is found in the _____."

Five Ways to Use the
Now I Know My Alef Bet Wall Poster

1 *Laminate and hang or mount on foam core* if you don't have permanent wall space. You may want to mount the poster on the door. Build excitement and anticipation for children as they enter the classroom. Put some kind of frame around or arrow to the letter of the day. Each week, as students enter the class, you can ask, "Can you find today's Hebrew letter?"

2 *Use the large poster to review the letters and key vocabulary* by asking the following kinds of questions. "Name the letters on all the children wearing yellow/blue/green shirts." "Can you name the Hebrew words on all the boys'/girls' shirts?" "Who remembers what letter we learned last week?" "I'm looking for someone holding an *lulav.*" "Point to the girl holding the *bayit.*" "Who can find four things that belong in the Beit K'nesset? *Torah, ner tamid,* etc." "Who is ready for Hanukkah?" "What two children are holding things for Sukkot?" "Which children are holding things that grow?"

3 *Enlarge a set of stickers,* or if you have an extra set of stickers, put stickers on index cards. (Not all sticker words are on the poster. Check the list of key words.) Put cards/stickers in a jar, tin, hat or box. Pick out a card, hold it up and ask a student to match it to the same word on the poster. Alternately, call on a student to come and pick out a card and match it to the poster. If your student picks a shofar, he/she says "shofar" and finds the boy on the poster holding the shofar. Then you can ask "What letter is on his shirt?" Or make a set of letters from the Hebrew alphabet. Pull out a letter and ask someone to find a child holding something that begins with that letter (*lamed* for *lulav, mem* for *mezuzah*).

5 *Order an extra poster to cut up and create a series of games.*

[a] **Living Alef Bet Game.** Cut the poster into individual letters and arrange as a game board or laminate the letter/pictures together in one long strip. Have each student pick a number and move that many spaces. The student is to name the letter or word on the square he/she has landed on. Or call out a word. The first student to correctly point to the word may move to it.

[b] **Twister.** Cut the poster into individual letters and randomly place in an area. Call out a body part (arm, leg, nose) and a letter for a child. The child has to put a body part on that letter and hold the position until his/her next turn. For example, "Bobby, put you right leg on the letter *resh.* Brittany, put your left elbow on the *lulav.*"

5 *Make a box of alef-bet objects:* lulav, shofar, or tallit. Pull out an object and have a student find the same object on the poster. Or reverse the process. Point to something on the poster and have a student find it in the box. Items in the box need not be real. They can be pictures on cards or plastic symbols (e.g., a rose), or you can use this as an opportunity to make all kinds of neat stuff.

Five Ways to Use the Alef Parent Education Folders

1 *Have a parent open house at the beginning of the school year.* Walk through the Alef Curriculum and show off all the books they and their children will be using during the year. Investing parents in the process is the key to the Alef Curriculum. The goal is to excite parents. Their children will learn something. They will learn something.

2 *Invite parents into class for the last fifteen minutes of every session.* Plan a celebration on whatever topic you are studying. For the Rosh ha-Shanah lesson, have a shofar blowing contest and serve apples and honey; for the Torah lesson, open up the Torah and serve Torah cookies; for the Shavuot lesson, read the Ten Commandments and make blintzes or other dairy foods.

3 *Create a lending library of books.* Not every family will be able to get books suggested in the parent folders. Have students make book tags to label the books and have them available for checkout.

4 *Have a class newsletter that goes home either weekly or monthly.* It can include subjects such as: Over the last week/month we...; Topics covered; Words learned/said/written/overheard in class; Ask your child about...; Mitzvah opportunities; Our class needs or needs help with...; and Upcoming events. If a newsletter is too much to handle, add a monthly calendar of events to the parent folder. You can alert parents to upcoming Jewish holidays, the school calendar and other easy-to-access information.

5 *Carpool clue.* If students go home in a carpool that is not with their parents, write a letter for parents to give to the members of the carpool that urges them to be aware of the Alef booklets going home each week.

Five Ways to Use Jewish Values from Alef to Tav Stories in Your Classroom

1 *Values heroes:* Have parents and students scan the newspapers for values heroes. It might be easier to look for tzedakah heroes, but this is more interesting. Have students search for someone who had *emunah* (faith) that something would happen, displayed great *simḥah* (joy), or who refrained from *lashon ha-ra* (gossiping). Create a bulletin board of real values heroes and add new ones throughout the year. Have students share their articles when they bring them in to class.

2 *Values museum:* Create a class museum of values. You can use artwork, creative stories and poetry as your exhibit. Over the course of the year, your students can do individual and class projects in all kinds of creative arts. Some of your students will be better at words, and some will be better in art. Each child should create several pieces of art, articles, stories and poetry. At the end of the year, open the museum to parents and other classes. Students can act as docents and explain the exhibit as parents or other classes visit.

3 *Mitzvah values journal:* Help students integrate these new values into their lives by creating values journals. Have students regularly write in their journal things they are thinking about that touch the values they are studying. For example: I SHOWED *KAVOD* (HONOR) TO MY MOM. SHE BOUGHT ME THE WRONG KIND OF NOTEBOOK FOR SCHOOL. I WAS GOING TO YELL AT HER, BUT I DECIDED THAT I WOULD SHOW *KAVOD*. I TOLD HER THAT IT WAS NOT THE NOTEBOOK EVERYONE ELSE WOULD HAVE. SHE UNDERSTOOD AND GOT ME THE ONE I WANTED. THE LAST TIME THIS HAPPENED, I YELLED AT HER AND SHE WAS REALLY MAD AT ME. IT TOOK THREE DAYS BEFORE SHE WOULD SMILE AT ME. IT WAS GOOD TO SHOW *KAVOD* AND NOT YELL AT HER.

4 *Story books:* Have students write and illustrate either the stories in the values curriculum or new versions of the stories. Create hardcover books with cardboard on the outside and paper on the inside to fashion the book. Make the books about 8" x 8". Once they are completed you can have students reread the stories on their own (you may want to create a reading area) or share the books with younger classes.

5 *Values quilt (like the AIDS Quilt):* Make a quilt out of squares of decorated fabric. Either each student can choose which value he or she wishes to illustrate, or you can assign students to work on specific values. Once the squares are decorated, sew the pieces together and hang it. If you can find someone who does quilting, you may want to have it finished as a real quilt. The quilt can become a lasting memory and hang in a hallway or foyer of the school.

Five Ways to Use Marilyn Price & Friends Present the Alphabet from Alef to Tav in Your Classroom

1 *Hebrew names:* Reinforce Hebrew letters by creating versions of your students' names. Trace each student's Hebrew name on a piece of butcher paper and affix it to a bulletin board or to the wall. Each time you study a new letter, ask who has that letter in his or her Hebrew name. Those who have the newly introduced Hebrew letter in their names may decorate the traced area of that letter. They can use crayons, colored pencils or whatever is appropriate. Have a celebration every time a student completes his or her name. Alternatively, get a set of Hebrew letter beads. Students will be able to add a Hebrew letter when it is learned. When all the letters are learned, the student may wear the necklace with his or her name.

2 *Create an environment:* Create some alef-bet or vocabulary pillows—soft or stuffed letters—for the class. If you are handy, you may want to to make the pillows into the letter shapes. If not as handy, you can use transfer paper to add the letter to an existing pillow. During breaks or when students are finished with their work, they can play in the pillow area and work at recognizing letters or reviewing vocabulary. Or create a mobile of Hebrew letters to brighten the classroom. Use lightweight clay (such as Crayola Model Magic) and paint the letters bright colors. Perhaps each week it would be the responsibility of a student to make the new letter. As more letters are added, ask students to identify letters and perhaps tell one vocabulary word. Consider the finished projects as an addition to the classroom or principal's office.

3 *Vocabulary review:* Instead of wallpaper, cover a wall or go around the walls with vocabulary mini-posters. You can review vocabulary by moving around the classroom instead of holding cards up. Or shrink a set of vocabulary words and make several sets of "playing cards." Students can play Match Game or Name That Card games on their own.

4 *Puppets:* Marilyn Price's puppets are made from ordinary household materials. They take some ingenuity. Make a set of your own class puppets to review letters. Use whatever you have available and be creative.

5 *Felt board and letters:* Create a felt board and letters (or buy a felt board or letters) for the class. Make sure that there are letters and vowels included. Use it to help introduce new letters and vowels or allow students to come up and make letter and vowel combinations.

Bibliography

Adler, David A. *The Number On My Grandfather's Arm*. New York: UAHC, 1987.

Beiner, Stan. *Bible Plays*. Alternatives in Religious Education, Inc. Denver Colorado, 1988.

Beiner, Stan. *Sedra Scenes*. Alternatives in Religious Education, Inc. Denver, Colorado. 1982

Bigham, Vicki Smith, and George Bigham. *The Prentice Hall Directory of Online Education Resources*. Paramus, New Jersey: Prentice Hall, Inc., 1998.

Brophy. *Learning and Teaching*.

Bunting, Eve. *The Terrible Things: An Allegory of the Holocaust*. Jewish Publication Society, 1996.

Burgstahler, Sheryl. *New Kids on the Net, A Network Sampler: Internet Activities for K-12*. Needham Heights. MA: Allyn and Bacon, 1997.

Buscaglia, Leo F. *The Fall of Freddie the Leaf*. Holt, Rinehart and Winston, 1983.

Fay, Jim, and David Funk. *Teaching With Love and Logic: Taking Control of the Classroom*. Golden, CO: The Love and Logic Press, Inc., 1995.

Gellman, Marc. *Always Wear Clean Underwear, And Other Ways Parents Say "I Love You"*. New York. Morrow Junior Books, 1997.

Gellman, Marc. *Does God Have a Big Toe? Stories About Stories in the Bible*. Harper Collins, Inc., 1989.

Gellman, Marc. *God's Mailbox*. New York: Morrow Junior Books, 1996.

Gies, Miep. *Anne Frank Remembered: The Story of the Woman Who Helped to Hide the Frank Family*. Turtleback, 1988.

Ginsburg, Marvell. *The Tatooed Torah*. New York: UAHC Press, 1983.

Green, Irving. *Judaism on the Web*. IDG Books Worldwide. 1997

Grishaver, Joel Lurie, and Beth Huppin. *Tzedakah, Gemilut Chasadim & Ahavah: A Manual for World Repair*. Denver, CO. Alternatives in Religious Education, Inc., 1983.

Herman, Erwin. *The Yanov Torah*. Rockville, MD: Kar Ben Copies, 1985.

Hyman, Paula E., ed., and Deborah Dash Moore. *Jewish Women in America*. 1997.

Jaffe, Nina, and Steve Zeitlin. *While Standing on One Foot*. New York: Henry Holt and Company, 1993.

Klein, Gerda Weiss. *Promise of a New Spring*. Chappaqua, N.Y.: Rossel Books, 1981.

Kohn, Alfie. *Beyond Discipline: From Compliance to Community*. Association for Supervision and Curriculum Development, 1996.

Kohn, Alfie. Punished by Rewards: *The Trouble with Gold Stars, Incentive Plans, A's, Praise, and other Bribes*. Houghton, Mifflin Co., 1993.

Lanton, Sandy. *Daddy's Chair*. Rockville, MD: Kar-Ben Copies, Inc., 1991.

Levin, Michael. *The Guide to the Jewish Internet*. San Franciscon, CA. No Starch Press, 1996.

Lowry, Lois. *Number the Stars*. Laureleaf, 1998.

Marcus, Audrey Friedman, ed. *The Jewish Teachers Handbook, Volume III*. Denver, CO. Alternatives in Religious Education, Inc., 1982.

Masden, Sheila, and Bette Gould. *The Teacher's Book of Lists*. Glenview, IL: Good Year Books, 1994.

Melamed, Deborah M. *The Three Pillars: A Book For Jewish Women*. Women's League of the United Synagogue of America, 1927.

Olitzky, Kerry M., and Ronald H. Isaacs. *The How to Handbook for Jewish Living*. Hoboken, New Jersey. KTAV Publishing House, Inc. 1996.

Olitsky, Kerry M. and Ronald H. Isaacs. *The Second How to Handbook for Jewish Living.*Hoboken, New Jersey. KTAV Pulishing House, Inc. 1996

Orlich, Donald C., and Robert J. Harder, Richard C. Callahan, Constance H. Kravas, Donald P. Kanchak, R.A. Pendergrass, and Andrew Keogh. Teaching Strategies: A Guide to Better Instruction, 2nd Ed. Lexington, MA: D.C. Heath & Co., 1985.

Pipher, Mary. *Reviving Ophelia: Saving the Selves of Adolescent Girls*. N.Y. Putnam Publishers, 1994.

Pipher, Mary. *The Shelter of Each Other: Rebuilding Our Families*. N.Y Ballantine Books, 1997.

Pomerantz, Barbara. *Bubbe, Me, and Memories.*

Ramsey, Robert D. *The Principal's Book of Lists*. Paramus, N.J. Prentice Hall, Inc., 1996.

Raver, Miki. *Listen to Her Voice*. N.p.: Chronicle Books, ?

Romm, Diane. *The Jewish Guide to the Internet*. Northvale, N.J. Jason Aronson, Inc., 1996.

Roseman, Kenneth. *Escape from the Holocaust*. New York: UAHC, 1985.

Rossel, Seymour. *Managing the Jewish Classroom: How to Transform Yourself into a Master Teacher*. Los Angeles: Torah Aura Productions, 1987.

Sanford, Doris. *It Must Hurt A Lot: A Child's Book About Death.*

Saphier, Jon, and Mary Ann Haley. *Activators: Activity Structures to Engage Students' Thinking Before Instruction*. Carlisle, MA. Research For Better Teaching, 1993.

Saphier, Jon, and Mary Ann Haley. *Summarizers: Activity Structures to Support Integration and Retention of New Learning*. Carlisle, MA. Research for Better Teaching, 1993.

Sasso, Sandy Eisenberg, and Sue Levi Elwell. *Jewish Women: A Mini-Course*. Denver, Co. Alternatives in Religious Education.

Schram, Peninnah. *Tales of Elijah the Prophet*. Northvale, N.J. Jason Aronson, 1991.

Segal, Eliezer. *Uncle Eli's Special-For-Kids Most Fun Ever Under-The-Table Passover Haggadah*. N.p. 1999.

Stock, Gregory. *The Kids Book of Questions*. N.Y. Workman Publishing Company, 1988.

Telushkin, Joseph. *Words That Hurt, Words That Heal: How to Choose Words Wisely and Well*. N.Y. William Morrow & Co., 1996.

Thinker Task Cards. Good Apple Creative Thinking Activity Book, 1992

Volavkova, Hana, ed. *I Never Saw Another Butterfly*. Schocken Books, Inc. 1993

Wolfson, Ron. *The Art of Jewish Living:* Hanukkah. Federation of Jewish Men's Clubs, New York, 1990

Wolfson, Ron. *The Art of Jewish Living: A Time to Mourn, A Time to Comfort.* Federation of Jewish Men's Clubs, 1993

Wong, Harry K. and Rosemary Tripi Wong. *The First Days of School: How to be an Effective Teacher.* Harry K. Wong Publications, Sunnyvale, California. 1991

Zalben, Jane Breskin. Pearl's Marigolds. *For Grandpa.* Simon and Schuster. 1997

The Invisible Thread: A Portrait of Jewish American Women. Jewish Publication Society. 1989

Torah Aura Materials

Electronic

C.Ha. A weekly publication for grades 5-8.

Bim Bam A weekly publication for grades 8-12.

Instant Lessons:

Tales of Elijah the Prophet

Remember Me

Schindler's List

Trouble in Jewish Cheyenne

What If the Fiddler Stopped Fiddling?

The Red in My Father's Beard

Fifteen Steps to Freedom

The True Story of Hanukkah

Books

Jewish Parents: A Teacher's Guide by Joel Lurie Grishaver.

BJL Shabbat

BJL Hanukkah

Ox, House, Camel, Door

Alef Parent Education Folders

Madrikhim Handbook

Being Torah

A Sense of Shabbat

The Grey Striped Shirt

Video

"My Exodus"